"A psychedelic dreamworld metaphysical journey and spellbinding story of a life."—Cat Pleska, author of *Riding on Comets: A Memoir*

"Lyrical and radically fearless stories about suffering and revelations of beauty. You'll be spellbound in the current of a masterful storyteller."—Annie Woodford, author of *Where You Come from Is Gone: Poems*

"The essays in this stunning collection are elegiac, urgent, vulnerable—full of loss and longing. Although the narrative is rooted in Kentucky, the scope is global as the narrator travels literally and metaphorically toward love and away from the ghosts of the past."—Sue William Silverman, author of *Acetylene Torch Songs: Writing True Stories to Ignite the Soul*

"A great pleasure to read. These lyrical essays explore what it means to leave a place where one has deep familial roots and to travel far and wide, geographically and culturally, without ever escaping the pull of home and its mysteries, richness, and sadness."—Zoe Zolbrod, author of *The Telling: A Memoir*

"These lyrical sojourns soar through space and time—revisiting hollows, canyons, and holy rivers of the past—and holding them up to the light. McElmurray's prose traverses terrain both haunted and lush, faraway and deeply familiar, while surveying the boundaries of longing, possibility, and the physical and spiritual manifestations of home. A stunning collection of essays from a master of the form."—Sonja Livingston, author of *Ghostbread*

I Could Name God in Twelve Ways

I Could Name God in Twelve Ways

essays

Karen Salyer McElmurray

UNIVERSITY PRESS OF KENTUCKY

Published by The University Press of Kentucky, scholarly publisher for
the Commonwealth, serving Bellarmine University, Berea College, Centre
College of Kentucky, Eastern Kentucky University, The Filson Historical
Society, Georgetown College, Kentucky Historical Society, Kentucky State
University, Morehead State University, Murray State University, Northern
Kentucky University, Spalding University, Transylvania University, University
of Kentucky, University of Louisville, University of Pikeville, and Western
Kentucky University.

Editorial and Sales Offices: The University Press of Kentucky
663 South Limestone Street, Lexington, Kentucky 40508-4008
www.kentuckypress.com

Library of Congress Cataloging-in-Publication Data

Names: McElmurray, Karen Salyer, 1956- author.
Title: I could name God in twelve ways : essays / Karen Salyer McElmurray.
Description: Lexington, Kentucky : The University Press of Kentucky, 2024.
Identifiers: LCCN 2024009771 | ISBN 9781985900646 (hardcover) | ISBN
   9781985900653 (paperback) | ISBN 9781985900677 (pdf) | ISBN
   9781985900660 (epub)
Subjects: LCSH: McElmurray, Karen Salyer, 1956- | McElmurray, Karen Salyer,
   1956—Travel. | Women authors, American—Biography.
Classification: LCC PS3563.C35966 I33 2024
LC record available at https://lccn.loc.gov/2024009771

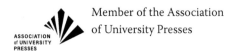

Member of the Association
of University Presses

ASSOCIATION
of UNIVERSITY
PRESSES

To Johnny, with whom I have shared these years with animals and a garden and love.

CONTENTS

PROLOGUE

Robyn Davidson's *Tracks* is her account of trekking 1,700 miles across the Australian outback with four camels and a dog. William Least Heat-Moon's *Blue Highways* is his thirteen-thousand-mile journey exploring American culture via diners and bars, fishing boats and factories. Annie Dillard's *Teaching a Stone to Talk* is a collection of fourteen personal essays set in the jungles of Ecuador, the Galápagos Islands, a church service, and a cottage in the Appalachian Mountains. These are among the many books that have taken me outside the parameters of my own skin, taken me to worlds not mine. All such books, and a dozen more on the shelves of my tiny study, are about traveling through worlds and seeking an ineffable something, be it in an unfamiliar geography or inside a self. In these days of divisive politics and the ravages of climate change, such traveling can seem, to say the least, like otherworldly luxury.

My first memory of travel is driving with my father and mother from Harlan County over the mountains on our way to eastern Kentucky. I remember my parents' quarrel words and the taste of saltines to still my stomach as we drove the windy roads. As our paths crossed and recrossed, I left my childhood behind, then longed for whatever it was that growing up had failed to give me. I lived in my grandmother's attic and went to college. I moved again and again, from town to town, state to state, lover to lover. "Go west, young woman," I told myself as I took a Greyhound back east. I drove all night on speed and caffeine, from Arizona to Kentucky. I inhabited this new town, that strange city, and then another one. I studied and took on the world by degrees. I was a lost girl, my shadow trailing behind me like a tattered mourning cloth. Then it was 1989, and I left the country with a young man named Paul, destination unknown; we had five hundred bucks hidden in our backpacks and no return tickets. These days, such a journey can seem like an exorbitant one, one of great privilege. The truth is, it was hard work. It was an untangling of who I'd been and who I wanted to be, and it was the story of my complete inability to find the center of that knot.

We worked grape harvests. Worked in factories. Waited tables. Bought cheap merchandise in one place to unload for a profit in another. Slept on beaches, beneath trees, and in ditches. I'd come from poor people, and my travels with Paul echoed that raising. We ate the food our wealthy patrons left behind in restaurants. We shoved stolen bread beneath our shirts. We tried on the masks of unfamiliar places, the guises of other people's lives, as if they could ever be our own. What did the people we met as we caught rides in Yugoslavia or squeezed into the buses in northern India think of us, a lean blond man with a giant backpack and a scrawny woman who wore sleeveless shirts even as we walked past a minaret and its call to prayer? Journeys were the masks of worlds I didn't understand any more than I understood my own sorrowing heart. We hitch-hiked and stowed away from England to France, Greece, Nepal, and India. I saved a red cloth from Thailand. Saved the sandstones I bought on the street in Agra. I saved the memory of frangipani. The memories of tastes and sounds and scents. My then lover and I came home with a box of slides, but they vanished inside the grief that followed the demise of our relationship. Memory was a hard teacher. Through it all, there was a paper trail. Notebook after notebook full of images of what I'd seen. Full of dreams. Full of small drawings of faces. Full of words.

These years later, summoning words has been my vocation. I have sat down to write about those years of traveling, but remembering has been complicated. What did Martine's shoes look like when we worked the grape harvest in France? Even when I remembered, I didn't think linearly. Traveling in a lorry from Ireland to England was then. Living in my grandmother's attic was also then. Times crossed and crisscrossed as I wrote over the several years these pages took. I didn't necessarily believe in words like *then* or *now*. This time was part of that time. That time transformed into this one, a veritable Gordian knot. Not to mention that, for me, *true to the bone* was part and parcel of *true to the heart*. The biggest question: What has traveling really meant, anyway?

In the end, traveling—be it as a teenager who left home at fifteen, as a twenty-something seeking places to come to rest, or as a thirty-year-old white woman hitching between countries—has meant *something*, and I offer that word here because there is no better one. The truth is, no one word suffices. Paul and I were exotic in our wandering and exotic in how we were seen. Once, in Kathmandu, a family asked us to sit with them and pose as someone took our photograph. Us, the floating American ghosts who seemed to have everything and, moreover, to be able to go anywhere. And still, with these pages, I seek reasons for all my wandering. Other words exist. *Spiritual enlightenment. Transcendence.* Or this something: the uncovering of a grief so far down inside me, thousands of miles weren't enough to escape its hold over my life.

I Could Name God in Twelve Ways is a collection of thirteen essays, ranging in times from the late 1970s to the late 1980s and early 1990s. They are about living with my granny in a house that once belonged to her mother, and her mother before her. The essays are about the blazing heat of summer in India. They are about Varanasi's holy river. They are set in the ghats and spirit houses of Bangkok. They visit a small island near Crete and a shrine to the Holy Mother. The vineyards of France and the mountains of northern Nepal. The essays follow the end of my love affair with Paul. Some essays are set in the early 2000s, during visits to see my mother in Prestonsburg, Kentucky, as her life unknitted with

Alzheimer's. One essay is set in 2018 in a psychiatric ward in Columbia, Maryland. There are creative writing classrooms. There's an attic in a generations-old house. *Here. There. Now. Then.* What, as Genghis Khan asks Marco Polo in Italo Calvino's *Invisible Cities*, is really the purpose of all this traveling?

I Could Name God in Twelve Ways is about deserts and unfamiliar oceans. It is about steep mountains reaching toward the sky, and it is about temples and marketplaces in exotic cities. It is also about home. While I traveled, I dreamed of the creosote bridge across the creek in front of my grandmother's house. In these essays, I take up words and arrange them on pages, much as my granny once cut cloth and made quilts with names like Trip around the World.

My word quilts, these essays, are blue and somber. They are hot yellow, unclouded suns. They are the blank white of an unpainted canvas. They are all colors, made of many years as well as now. My hope is to continue to unravel this journey, the story of this body in this time and place as well as in that one. I hope that the pages of this journey are honest about despair and humble in the face of wonder. These twelve lyric essays weave together place and memory and the present. Time has become a quilt made of poetic and particular prose. Time is both shadow and hope.

BLUE GLASS

1.

My hands are spread-fingered, palms up on the table. Lifeline, divided by an *x*. A scar in the shape of a half-moon. Hands like my mother's and her mother's before her. I turn these hands over and back, feeling their emptiness. I'm the only one in the break room besides a tall man in a tracksuit who nods at my paper pajamas and remarks that I must be new on 1 North. He tells me that tea will make me feel better, sets a cup in front of me, and says his name is Joshua. I sip, holding the hot liquid in my mouth while he tells me he's been here for three weeks. The burn travels from my tongue down my throat while he looks at me like he gets that I'm a raw nerve.

The night before in the emergency room, they gave me an Ativan-filled IV, so sleep had a hallucinatory vagueness through which I remember orderlies rolling a gurney down a hallway and someone shouting the same words over and over: "Oh my God, oh my God." The nurses were talking about delirium tremens. I imagined an empty Four Roses whiskey bottle lying in a ditch beside some abandoned house. I begged them to admit me.

Joshua's leaving this afternoon, he says as I take another sip of the tea and swallow, feeling heat dissolve in my chest. I am afraid to cry, knowing I might never stop.

2.

Late winter 2018 had meant a near house fire, long cold weeks, and no electricity or heat in our home. Back in Kentucky, my mother's death was imminent. Dying too, the yellow cat named Earl, who lay at the foot of my bed, eyeing me with a trust I couldn't fathom. "Poor me," I told myself. "Get some pluck. Some get-up-and-go." I walked blocks past the piles of blackened snow in the neighborhood, listening to my breath. I commuted two hours north for my part-time teaching gig at a small, wealthy college where I doubted my shoes, my accent, my educational pedigree. Back home, I sat by the small gas stove in our living room, swathed in blankets as I tried one more time to revise the novel I'd worked on for so long. Snow fell for hours, a steady, quiet momentum I couldn't possibly match. I layered on blankets and quilts and lay in bed, the dog huddled at my side, whimpering her worry. All that winter, I tried to locate the source of the doubt that ran like a thin cold river through my heart. "I'm sorry for your suffering," a friend said when I called her. I laughed. Isn't suffering the reason for great art?

3.

1 North. Howard County General Hospital. Columbia, Maryland. I spent eleven days there, admitted early on the morning of April 23, 2018, with severe General Anxiety Disorder. I was, at the time of my admittance, recorded as female, Caucasian, five feet, four inches tall, one hundred thirty-five pounds, sixty years old, typical blood pressure 110 over 72, standard body temperature 98.9, unknown blood type. Married. History of two pregnancies—one termination by abortion, one relinquishment to adoption via Kentucky Department of Social Services—presently postmenopausal. My medical history showed a history of colorectal cancer, in remission. Ménière's syndrome, accompanied by major hearing loss in right ear. History of bronchitis and evidence of lung nodules, possibly connected to past residence in the coal mine regions of eastern Kentucky. Metal rod in right ankle because of a car accident in 1999. Small lipoma, middle of right arm. Seasonal allergies. Marked history of depression over

a period of thirty-some years, treated most often via general practitioners and clinical social workers. One admission to a public facility for depressive crisis after relationship dissolution. At the time of my current breakdown, I had been treated over the years with a variety of psychotropic drugs, including Prozac, Zoloft, Celexa, Cymbalta, Effexor, and, over the last seven-plus years, Lexapro. At my first psychiatric evaluation, a young woman named Dr. X makes notes on my medical history. Upside down on the paper she's filling out, I see some words, one of which is *vulnerable*.

4.

Fear sat inside my chest, kicking its little legs against my heart. The fear was stubborn and resistant to everything I tried—sleep, cold showers, Valium. I feared writing, not writing. My mother had been in a nursing home with Alzheimer's for almost seven years, and I feared her imminent death at the same time I wanted her to pass on. Two months before, I'd fallen and injured the iliotibial band in my right leg, and the needle-sharp pain alternated with the lead weight of anxiety, a distraction I needed.

I was standing on an edge, ready to plummet into the dark space inside me, but I somehow knew that place. It was a well I remembered from when I was small. My granny's hands were ropy with veins as she fed shirts through the wringer washer. I sniffed the soap scent of wet sheets in the basket and followed behind her. More shirts and towels were drying, clean and stiff, on the long clothesline near the garden, and there she dumped the water near the tomato plants. At the well, she shooed me back. She hooked the handle of the bucket on a rope and cranked as I peered into the deep mossy damp, thick with the muck scent of sulfur. I was lowering now, the taste of that rope in my mouth as anxiety consumed me, inch by inch.

The well of myself was as dark as the childhood one, and dark was the only place I felt safe. I pulled the covers over my head at six o'clock, waiting for the hours before dark to pass. I drank cups of chamomile tea, took the drugs doctors doled out. *Klonopin. Propranolol. Trazodone.* I awoke after four hours' sleep, begging my husband to do something, take me somewhere. *Hospital.* "What would they do if we took you there?" John asked, his face helpless. I longed for the bottom of the well, that blank, black space where I could lie down and be invisible once and for all.

5.

To be *vulnerable*, the definitions say, is to be delicate. Broken. We are all vulnerable in one way or another, my associates and I on 1 North. I don't know if *associates* describe what we are, but other words jar just as much. Peers? The other inpatients? We are not quite friends. Donna, the thirty-something woman from the homeless shelter, is here for oxycodone addiction. Her lips look vulnerable as she eats one of the mini powdered-sugar doughnuts John brings me. Her review—with two psychiatrists from Howard General, plus a social worker and a court rep—is coming up soon, though she is not yet sure if the group home will work out for her. Syd is also delicate. She's the twenty-year-old in for post-alcoholism treatment and recurring anorexia. At lunch in the break room, the aides tell Syd she must eat, eat, and she tears off tiny corners of her sandwich and hides them underneath her plate. In group therapy, Syd sits under the blanket from her room and draws big-eyed women with one of the crayons we're allowed to use. None of us are allowed things that dangle, have sharp edges or points, or tie tightly. Each afternoon, I ask to use the red ink pen I brought to finish the term's essay grading with, though it soon grows evident that I have surrendered far more than the pen. My head swirls with words, querulous little birds made of broken lines and circles that used to be letters. My roommate, Jojo, loves to draw, though on her first morning she had to surrender a set of brightly colored pencils. One afternoon I wake from a nap to find her huddled beneath the sheets, crying. I sit beside her and stroke her beautiful auburn hair, which she says has grown thinner with all the medications. She is on a suicide watch, she tells me as sunlight comes between the curtain panels and trails along the floor. Strands of dust blow from the filthy heating vents.

6.

As I talked to them about art, students glanced at their phones or studied the wall clock. I read them passages from Flannery O'Connor, who lived for twelve years after a diagnosis of systemic lupus. She went back to the family farm in Milledgeville, Georgia, and is said to have written facing a wall, her feet in a bucket of ice water. "The basis of art," she said, "is truth, both in matter and in mode." Each day that spring, I read the students some snippet about truth. How we create from our experiences. How fear is often the basis for creativity. Look at van Gogh. Think of the almond blossoms and *The Yellow House*. Think of his sky full of stars. Hands went up. Someone asked about his ear, and someone else asked how he'd died. The room emptied as van Gogh's final words came to me: "The sadness that will last forever."

7.

"Sometimes it rains all day, and sometimes it just rains." My mother said this when there was the kind of rain that starts early of a morning and keeps on, steady and gentle, into all the afternoons outside our subdivision house. Rain, she said, used to be so pure. She told me how she used to catch rain in a wash pan for her hair, to make it soft. I remember seeing her hair in brush curlers and loose strands fanning her face in the morning sun.

The mother I later wrote was a woman bitter and afraid of the world. Her face, peering out from behind the drawn curtains of our house. Her fear of who might be knocking on the door, who might have just pulled up in the driveway. The world that soiled our bodies was to be cast out: the mud trapped on the soles of shoes walking across our floors, the dark marks stray fingers could make on a wall. The world was not welcome. And those other fears. The things we do to call down the wrath of the Lord. Desire. Pleasure. All those unclean human longings, human acts, those touches of a human hand. Did not the mouth of God open and spew forth both wrath and pity? Oh, small humans that we are, full of the frailty of want. Were not his holy words about our uncleanliness before the radiance of heaven? Our house could never be clean enough, no matter how much we polished it with our sadness.

8.

Vulnerable. A woman is admitted to 1 North to wean off her medication. She stays in bed for days, her face toward the closed curtains. *Vulnerable.* Travon, the beautiful Haitian boy who never says a word and curls up to sleep on the tile floor during group sessions. *Vulnerability.* Graham, in for heroin addiction, his lean body sequestered between Donna and Syd, who both want him, bad. *Vulnerability.* Shayk, just finishing a two-month stint on 1 North as he gets his bipolar disorder under control. He shows me photographs of his one-year-old daughter, with her mother in Florida. He plays me computer-generated songs he's written about mania. *Vulnerability.* Raina, who never leaves her room after the fistfight she started with Donna, whom she knows from the homeless shelter. *Vulnerability.* Tina, the tiny eighty-year-old woman who sits rocking her upper body over and over and over by the break room window that gives the most sunlight. *Vulnerable.* Myself one afternoon when George, the psychiatric nurse, breaks a ward rule and comes into my room, where I'm taking a nap. He stands two feet from my bed and tells me how much better I'm looking today and how much he likes my hair. *Vulnerable.* Vivya, who uses her crayons to draw stick figures—one stick person holding its stick arms out toward two tiny stick children. Vivya sits with her legs up in a chair, picking at the calluses on her feet as she tells me that the antipsychotic Navane has helped her release these ghost children, the ones she longs for and has never been able to have.

9.

The women I'm from wore vulnerability, the signs of it, on their bodies, if you knew exactly where to look. The broken lifeline on a palm. The thrice-split lip. That bruise around an eye. Empty arms that ached or hands that were rough from all the cleaning up one more time. The kind of vulnerability I'm talking about had a bite to it, a stinger you couldn't pull out. Things to fear were both palpable and not. They were spirits in your house, ghosts released by mirrors broken in the hallway, parts of your own body you should have controlled but didn't. "You know she could have done something about it if she'd wanted to," my grandmother said about my second cousin, whose father is in prison for having sex with her. Women were vulnerable, period. Made that way, the good book said. "So the Lord God caused a deep sleep to fall upon the man, and he slept; then He took one of his ribs and closed up the flesh at that place. And the Lord God fashioned into a woman the rib which He had taken from the man, and brought her to the man." Women, an appendage who should behave accordingly. What these women were, I have taken unto myself, worn like an unguent that neither healed nor soothed. Vulnerability has been my disguise, my go-to in times of doubt. There I am, thirty years old and a waif at one hundred pounds, wearing my itty-bitty green dress as I stand at the edge of the writing program get-together or wait my turn at the end of the cash bar. Why, you could go anywhere with a woman like me in your back pocket, and I would seem to like it just fine, the being left behind after last call or by my lonesome the next morning, my mouth tasting all forlorn. Even with that good, kind man, my friend, my husband. "Kiss me goodnight," I say. "Tell me why you love me, because surely you don't. Not me. Why, look at my words on the page, this page, the one after that. How dark these words are, how forsaken. Words that take you to the bottom of the well, to the rawest truth. With words as vulnerable as these," I say, "surely, surely you'll know the secret." "Of what?" he asks. "The secret of what?"

10.

Once when I led a nonfiction workshop as a visiting writer, I read them a passage from my memoir, then talked about my process and the need for vulnerability. I chose a section of the book that describes the day my son was born, my experience of becoming a mother and yet not one, after his surrender to adoption. I read and did what I do best—lost myself in the memory, the words, the flow of thought to thought to thought. A fugue state, one of the workshop members said. A kind of ecstatic detachment. I talked about diving into experience, being willing to show the beating heart, the wound. But it's like you've gone outside the words, outside your own body even, someone else said. It's like you're floating and don't know where to land. Is that what vulnerable means? Vulnerable, I said, turning the word over in my mouth, seeking the way to send it out into the room, true to my experience. I took a long drink of the soda I'd brought with me, feeling the paper straw fill and deflate in my mouth. I thought of how vulnerable a day of writing could be, my fear of the day after, the fear of having nothing left to say.

11.

On 1 North, eleven six-thirty wake-up calls. Eleven visiting hours from seven to eight thirty, eleven morning goal settings, eleven evening goal reviews, eleven breakfast trays and lunch trays and supper trays, eleven cold showers to jar myself awake. Eleven days to see what works best: Lexapro, Valium, Xanax, Klonopin, Atarax, Buspar, trazadone, Remeron, Abilify. Eleven days of ice from the machine, the same magazines, a locked glass door to a bench in a garden where no one goes. Eleven days of laps past the glassed-in office, past the kitchenette, past the conference rooms, past the break room, past the bedrooms with their always-open doors, past my room, and around again. Eleven days of group therapy, mornings and afternoons, where we talk about what we think we can't do and what we can. And there are other numbers. "Warning," a handout reads. "Symptoms of Inner Peace, One through Twelve." On the seventh day, I spend two hours in the afternoon with a nurse and an enema. She spreads a towel and tells me to lie down, to relax, and I tell her that this makes me anxious and that anxiety is why I'm here in the first place. "I'm a nurse," she says, "and I've seen everything." Her hand eases the tube up my rectum, and lukewarm water flushes inside as I hold my knees in my arms. On the ninth of the eleven days, I am one step ahead of my anxiety. I am more numb than vulnerable, more vulnerable than any words can describe. I am rocking in my chair just a little, just enough to feel my blood shake and stir, enough to know I'm still here.

12.

One of the last years I taught creative writing at the small Southern College, there was a new president. I remember the welcoming banquets and teas. She wore her hair in a stiffly sprayed bob, and her pantsuits were flowing and comfortable and just right with their navy blues and ironed shirts and smart jackets. I told myself I envied her, how she made her way through a room, shaking hands. When I met her, she gripped my fingers, her hand warm, her eyes sussing out who was next in the reception line and who was after that. I wondered if she was nervous. Come Friday, end of the first week, there was a convocation, and the president delivered her opening address. There were promises about vision, about new directions, about balance between the demands of our student customers and our lives as educators. And woven throughout the speech were admissions: "I'm not sure about any of this yet. I don't yet know about that." She admitted to us that what she felt as she took up the reins of her job was a strong measure of uncertainty. A colleague nudged me and shook his head in disappointment. "Never," he said, "admit your vulnerabilities."

13.

The most vulnerable I ever saw my mother was when she and I waited all day for my father to come home. It was Thanksgiving. He was at the office working, anything not to be with her and the arguments that ignited, that went on for hours, burning us alive. My mother was the Queen of Cleanliness, keeping my body, the house, her marriage all spotless. She bathed me until I was thirteen, and I more than once saw her lead my shamefaced father undressed through the house, paper bags taped to his feet, on his way to being sanitized after work. We were her subjects, my father and I, in her kingdom of order. By five o'clock that Thanksgiving, she watched his car round the corner, her perfectly made-up face betraying a loneliness and despair I never heard her admit.

I have translated this moment—that look on my mother's face— into essays, novels, a memoir, all of them in some way about being lost in a mire of past and present, confusion and anger. I have written from the vantage point of a street-smart, pregnant runaway. I have written from my own vantage point as a forty-something woman who is trying to understand the surrender of her son to adoption when she was fifteen years old. In my first novel, I wrote from the point of view of a young man who struggles to accept his sexual identity within the confines of a fundamentalist family. In my second novel, I wrote from the point of view of an older man who, having lost his son to a Marine Corps helicopter accident, goes on a soul's journey to find peace. In another novel, I wrote from the point of view of the daughter of a fortune teller who was shot and killed by someone who might have been her father. In all my work, my language is, as a friend said, *beautiful pain.* Raw. Almost too much to bear.

I've never called myself vulnerable, though I have in the last few years lost friendships for as much. A writer friend with whom I wrote letters for a blog ended our connection because of my propensity for anxiety. Another friend of many years severed our ties because of my neediness. Still, I would not call myself vulnerable. I am in some ways the opposite. Vulnerable. *The quality of being weak and easily hurt physically or emotionally.* I have these qualities, but into the well that is my life, I've cast enough dimes and nickels to ensure luck for at least the next quarter century.

My history of Rules for Self: Shut the right doors carefully, before too much or someone gets in. Ride the roads, usually alone, and turn the radio up loud. Wield shovels, picks, trowels, sledgehammers, and wedges with all the force you can muster. Lock eyes with the drummer in the band across the dance floor. Change lanes back and forth as you flirt recklessly with some truck driver who follows your turn signal into a rest stop, then drive away fast. Claim as many lovers as you can. Switch towns or states when intimacy becomes a difficult issue. Remain untouched at all costs, at least in the ways that count. Set firm boundaries—walls if necessary— around that territory called the heart. "Can you take it, baby?" a redneck lover asked me once as I knelt in front of him beside the boat at the river. For years I did just that. I swallowed all the hurt and came back for more.

Is being invulnerable the same as having a steel fence inside? Is being vulnerable the same as being weak? Vulnerability is not weakness, says research professor and storyteller Brené Brown. It is the birthplace of love, belonging, joy, courage, empathy, and creativity. It is the source of hope, accountability, and authenticity. If we want more meaningful spiritual lives, Brown goes on to say, vulnerability is our path. Fresh off the group discussion on 1 North, I am thinking about these very words as I lie down in my room. Jojo, my roommate, likes the curtains drawn fast, but they're not large enough to cover the long expanse of windows above the heating register. Hooks have fallen off at the center, and the curtains are parted, fingers of light crossing the bed as I try to sleep.

14.

My mother passed away in the spring after my breakdown. She had Alzheimer's, a disease made of stages of vulnerability. The first time I realized how ill she was, I was seeing her again after not visiting for almost a year. She came to the door to greet me, her polyester pants torn, her hair in knots. Another time I took her to the beauty shop, and she stood on the sidewalk, screaming no when I tried to take her inside. Her body grew more vulnerable as she unlearned food. But she was a longtime lover of chocolate. I remember her look of sheer delight when I put a Rebecca Ruth chocolate buckeye in her mouth, the way she took the chocolate out and gently stroked her face with it. I remember the gradual letting go of the way tastes—sweet, sour, bitter—distinguished themselves. Mashed potatoes were the same as chili when you pureed it. Ice, the same as hot soup. I remember the beautiful curve of her lips as I fed her, spooned carrots into her mouth. Mouth scraped, eyes wiped free of sleep, legs nurse lifted to accommodate a new diaper. The intent look in her eyes as she swallowed, defecated, peed, slept, all states of the body along one long continuum of waiting.

15.

Every night on 1 North, there's Alcoholics Anonymous. I don't belong in AA, I tell myself, but the meetings tell us that our paths toward peace are the same, regardless of who we are. Twelve steps. *Fearlessness. Shortcomings. Consciousness.* I can never remember all of the steps, but while Syd talks about the connection between her eating disorder and drinking, I count other twelves. Topeka; Allen; Frankfort; Hagerhill; Berea; Flagstaff; Charlottesville; Asheville; Athens, Lynchburg; Rome; Milledgeville: twelve towns I lived in before I was forty, discounting all the other back roads and side roads and waysides. Or lovers: Jim, Wayne, Steve, Michael, Tom, Otis, Peter, Rick, Paul, Dave, Fred, Eric, and so forth and so on, as the first twelve names spill from my lips. But naming—one and two and three toward twelve—doesn't mean very much after a while. The group leader says to think of it as Twelve Steps to Peace. I think of books read on sleepless nights. I think of twelve ways sorrow or pity or shame can be evoked, all without the complexities of the heart. Figs eaten right from the tree. The remembered scents of hands and mouths. Hot summer nights and porches I've left behind. Prayers said in sincerity. The number of times I heard my mother laugh like she meant it. After the meetings those nights on 1 North, I get in bed and count moments and fall asleep before I reach the number twelve.

16.

"What would it look like," Ken, the 1 North counselor, asks me at a group session, "if you didn't write at all? If you didn't define yourself by writing but by something else altogether?" I'm sitting next to Jojo, and I'm wrapped up in my blanket. Awake since five and lulled by an Atarax, I'm trying hard not to float away from the question, which seems to have come out of Ken's mouth like a small blackbird landing on my chest, trying to reach inside my sweatshirt, inside my tired skin. "Who are you," Ken asks, "besides what you write?" Inside my head is a montage of moments involving words. I see myself at fourteen, high on speed and up all night writing and drawing in a notebook full of not-good poems about love and hurt. I see myself at forty, standing in front of an audience that includes my son, his adoptive mother, a hiring committee, and a whole slew of writers and want-to-be writers there to listen to my memoir. I see myself in bed this winter, notebook paper wadded up or folded or torn into neat shreds around me. I see myself this very morning, standing by the glass doors in the break room, wondering if it will rain. *Stories. Essays. Lines from a novel.* What if there was nothing really but the rain landing in my palms and the coolness and the shine against my skin. "What does hope look like?" Ken asks.

17.

On the morning of day eleven, there's a cloud cover outside that promises not to break. Ken goes from one to the next of us, the ones who'll be leaving soon, to ask us how we are. Donna will be moving back to the group home, and she is worried that she will be sharing the space with three other women and with Raina, whom she has avoided since the fistfight. Syd says she ate toast and eggs for breakfast this morning and didn't want a drink afterward. And Jojo, my roommate. She says she just learned from her doctor this morning that she isn't quite ready yet to leave, that she needs several more days of staying put. "And you?" Ken asks. I'm sitting with my feet propped up on an end table. Fear isn't racing around inside me, but it's still there, flicking its tiny fingers against the inside of my chest cavity. I take a long drink of water from my plastic cup, remind myself to breathe.

18.

Since my time on 1 North, I keep a new journal. Remembered
dreams. Tastes and scents and textures. I try to make lists of beautiful things. Pink yarrow blooming on a hill. The orange tail of a fox I
glimpsed on my morning walk, the way the fox slipped like a wraith
into the thicket. The moments I lace my fingers through the hair on
my husband's chest, let my palm rest against him, feeling his blood
coursing. The other morning, amid these moments of beauty, I wrote
down the names of the dead. My mother, Pearlie Lee. Her mother,
also Pearl. Other ancestors. Ruby. Ruth. Stella. Leroy. The names
fill the margins of my journal, bring heft and weight to this page
full of beauty. There are parts of sentences, too. *A feather drifted
down from the branch and. A shower fell from the live oak after the
rain and I.* I worry about finishing these sentences, worry about
how beauty might become sentimentality. I wonder if vulnerability might leave an opening through which God knows what might
find its way. Then, not long ago, I rediscovered a page in the back
of the journal, a drawing from back on 1 North, the day after John
snuck watercolor pencils in and Jojo sat up all night drawing. The
drawing is bright with colors. Red. Orange. Vivid green and silver
and yellow. It is a girl's drawing, full of clear signs and wishing, and
I love it for that most of all. It's a drawing of a palm with an eye at
its center, the fingertips reaching for a heart.

19.

On my third morning out of 1 North, I am at a grocery store with
John. The vegetable area is full of tables laden with broccoli, apples,
potatoes. Soon, the signs promise, it will be spring. Overhead lights
hum in my ears, and I feel the medication I've been taking trembling

on the surface of my skin, and a grocery cart with a kicking child in it barely misses the back of my ankles. I want to hurry to my room, pull the covers over my head, and wait for my lunch tray, but this is it. The world is no longer out there but here, outside me and inside me too, and I can hardly breathe. I shove my hands in my pockets and stand still, shut my eyes, will myself to like it, this place too full of everything. The hand in my right pocket finds a piece of paper, and I take it out, hold it in my palm. The paper is folded and refolded into the kind of chain I used to make with gum wrappers when I was a kid. I unfold it, smooth the half sheet out on the edge of a scale by the bananas. It's a discussion topic from a group meeting: *What does it mean to be vulnerable both to others and to ourselves?*

20.

Once, I was part of a panel at a huge writers' conference with Dorothy Allison, a fierce woman writer I have always admired. She talked about risk, telling our audience that to write deeply—to, as she said, have our work be worth a damn—we must be willing to reach inside ourselves for our hardest-earned truths. We must be willing to open up our stories, and ourselves, to both pain and terror. I try to write such stories. Eleven days on a psych ward. Nine years teaching creative writing. Eighteen years learning to love my partner. Five days in front of a blank screen. Such experiences have a high cost, Dorothy Allison said. Some days, I glimpse cost. I see the half-moon scar on my third finger, and I remember my mother's hands, how a nail on her ring finger was torn away in an accident when she was a girl. A girl hurt already in ways I will never know, beyond repair already on her way to becoming a woman. A woman silenced, her vulnerabilities never named, never released. She has been dead six months now, set free at last from years of Alzheimer's suffering.

When my mother was a girl, she walked across a swinging bridge that spanned a river on her way to school each morning. I see her standing on one bank, looking across at the other, wondering how long rope and wood can hold up against time. I think of her as I look at the blue bottle that has hung on a tree in my garden all winter. Come summer, I try to read the fine scratches on the glass like a language I still have years to learn. What language did my mother understand at the end of her life? She had unremembered words for years, but I have to believe that somewhere inside her, written someplace as secret as the inside of her eyelids, she had discovered words all her own, ones none of us know, at least now.

And me? I have come to know the precariousness of it, the swinging bridge between calm and fear. Vulnerable, my medical records from 1 North called me. "Make lists of the things for which you are grateful," the healers there said. I write it down, the way light falls against the scarred wood floor. On the sunflower in my garden, the wings of the monarch are already raggedy at the start of summer. Beauty is hard earned. It is vulnerable and true. And so I write the child I was, in my mother's shadow before I had even begun to know what light meant. I write the young woman I became, hungry for the next road out. I write the woman I am, her spirit some days full of holes. Somewhere between meanness and beauty is a place called vulnerable, and if we are lucky, we learn to ride through that country, all the windows down and the wind in our faces, telling us we are alive.

THE ROADS SHE'S TRAVELED

When I wanted to be alone, I took my notebook along the dirt path, made my way past what used to be a hogpen, and climbed the hill behind Fannie Ellen's house. I was twenty years old, and I needed solitude, though I wouldn't understand why for years. All I knew was that my childhood had nearly eaten me alive. At sixteen, I'd given up my son for adoption, and since then I'd partied hard, filling up my emptiness with grief and confusion. Now I was trying a different life on for size: moving to eastern Kentucky to live with my granny in Johnson County while I attended Prestonsburg Community College. As I climbed the hill through a sting of briars, I named trees. *Sycamore. Chestnut. Tree of heaven.* The sound of the wind in those trees was holy.

At the top of the hill was a rock cliff, where I sat looking out over the whole wide world. Across from Fannie Ellen's lived distant cousins. Sue, married to Clifford, a laid-off miner. Faye and Alvin, who owned the country store. In my notebook I drew maps of that world. *Jenny's Creek. Bull Creek. Puncheon. Water Gap. Abbott Mountain.* Highway 1428 cut its way through the valley toward Floyd County, where my mother and all my maternal relatives lived. Another granny. My pa. The aunts and uncles and cousins—all of them fine for a visit, but none of them offered me a home. Home was far away, deep down and unseen. I got close to it by living with Fannie Ellen and by visiting Bear Holler, the abandoned farm where she'd been raised.

Fannie Ellen and I had walked that land more than once. She taught me how to know greens. *Poor Man's Bacon. Creasy. Dock.* She taught me about wishes, since Bear Holler had been the place of her girlhood dreams. She'd wanted to be a nurse, an ambition she gave up when she chose to marry my granddaddy. Home became roof and porch, became good men and good women, a fine line of distinction between them. Good men looked after their households, she said, and their women rose up at daylight and prepared their families in the ways of the Lord. I had no idea what *good* meant, but I'd tried for as long as I could remember to figure it out. My beliefs were books—everything from girl mysteries to Russian novels and the histories of martyred saints. As far as I could tell, God was made of thunderstorms, art, and the stories I knew about the women I came from. Strong women. Granny women. Even a bearded woman who ran off to join a traveling carnival. *Armentia George. Exer. Nethaladia. Ida Mae.* I kept their names in my notebook.

I wasn't a woman yet, and I sure wasn't good. I slipped out at midnight and drove over to Prestonsburg and Dewey Lake to swim with the boys I'd met at Dairy Cheer. I went dancing up at Pikeville, at Marlow Country Palace. I took rides in a coal rig with a boy named Little Boots, who taught me how to shift gears. I was always ready for a fight, as ready to head off into some big city as I was to stay put in Hagerhill. I had an idea of the woman I wanted to become, but most days I was a misfit. I was a stone rattling around in an empty Mason jar. As the sun slipped over the valley, I held my notebook close and studied a world I wanted badly to understand.

* * *

I left Hagerhill and went on to this college and that. I earned one degree, another. I gave myself away to an artist named Tom, then lived for a few years with a woman named Margaret, who tried to help me find my way back. I put love behind a wall I couldn't climb and told myself I felt nothing at all. I filled notebook after notebook with words and sentences and remembered dreams. I dreamed about crossing the creosote bridge in front of Fannie Ellen's house. I dreamed of the stone foundations of my great-grandparents' house up Bear Holler. I wrote stories and poems. I threw my hat in the ring for jobs and conferences and publications. And I always went back, sleeping or awake, to the land of my ancestors. I was forty years old, and I drove the long miles like they were hunger. I craved eastern Kentucky like it was the one good meal that could finally satisfy me.

In Floyd County, my mother was in the final stages of Alzheimer's. Granny and Pa, the aunts and uncles, they were gone too. There were still cousins, but I hardly knew them, and the Pentecostal Holiness Church across Highway 114 near my mother's house had become a car sales lot. In Hagerhill, Fannie Ellen was in nursing care, where she would pass at ninety-two. It was hard to see where any of it used to be, with her house and the hill I'd climbed all lying beneath new Route 23. I stayed as many days as I could on trips back, trying to hold that world on my tongue like it was Communion. It was an odd holiness. When I tried to walk up Bear Holler a blonde-headed woman came out of a house at the mouth of the hollow. Her eyes narrowed. A shirtless man in cowboy boots picked up a fist-sized rock and aimed it at me. At my mother's nursing home, a blind one-hundred-year-old woman looked out over the empty dining room tables. "Lord, honey," she said. "Look what they done to them mountaintops."

* * *

During those years, I gathered memories I could tell about the world I'd left behind. A short story was about a girl named Mary Ruth who worked at Murphy's Five and Dime. She loved working at night, winding up all the musical jewelry boxes and dreaming of other towns. I wrote about a collector of dolls, about a lover of snakes and Jesus, about a man who painted the walls of his house with images from the book of Revelation. The women I wrote drifted through the world as much as I had. Leah, a runaway, panhandled on a St. Louis street corner when she felt her baby's heartbeat for the first time. These stories of a floating world grew bigger. Leah became a memoir. My first novel was about a woman named Ruth Blue, who believed more in visions of angels than she did her own son's life. In another novel, Miracelle Loving traveled from Fairbanks to Miami, telling false fortunes. The women I wrote were uncertain of their lovers, their homes, their next meals. They rode miles toward futures they couldn't see, hitched rides along strange highways. Their journeys seemed to have no beginning, no middle, no end, and I let them wander, seeking exactly who they might someday become.

* * *

The women who have inhabited my prose—Leah, Sarah, Ruby, Ruth, Pearl, Lory, Miracelle—have kept a toehold on belonging in the world. Their stories have been about grief and rage. About loss and hurt. About seemingly insurmountable damage. If there's a common denominator for these women, one word—*journey*—covers it best. The women on my pages have traveled the stumbles of dirt paths, the perimeters of rooms in houses they seldom leave. They have inhabited spaces they struggle to escape, be they the heads of hollows or the confines of their own hearts. Some readers find the women I have written helpless. "Why," they want to know, "don't they just *get on with it*?" Once I wrote a character who spent a long night grieving the lover who had just slapped her across the face and kicked her out of a bar. As she walked across the parking lot, she tripped and fell and sat staring at a fistful of dirt. "What," a workshop peer wanted to know, "is all this silly business about dirt?"

I find the women I have written more held fast than helpless. They are fierce fighters, whether the fight is inside themselves or out. They have been beset by distances. They long for roads that will take them nowhere as much as they long for ones that might take them back home. They try mightily to find the selves they've lost or never had in the first place.

* * *

A few summers ago when I visited Kentucky, I rented a room at Jenny Wiley State Park. I rode around town, had a meal at Billy Ray's Restaurant and then took 114, the old road beside what used to be my mother's house. A planter sat on the porch next to the metal chair my pa used to sit in, whittling cedar. A car in the driveway belonged to this cousin or that one, not a one I really knew. I was lonely, but I needed silence. Come afternoon, I hiked in the park and climbed a hill to the unmarked grave of a soldier's wife. Beyond me was a blur of ridge and lake and, beyond that, an empty expanse of rutted hills. It began to rain, so back at the lodge, I sipped wine at the karaoke bar and sang along to easy-listening country until that left me wanting my room and a bed and bad television movies. In my burrow of sheets and blankets, the cold from the open balcony doors touched my face. *Just sleep now*, a voice said. *Sleep and see what you can see.* Like that, the stories I hadn't found all day found me.

"Your stories are like dreams," a friend once said of my writing, and so it was. Mist became a ghost shape, a ghost became a body, and Fannie Ellen stood beside my bed. Her veiny hands reached for mine. "Follow me," she said, and I did. We stepped through the balcony doors onto the red tile of her kitchen floor, and we stood by the window, looking up at the hill I used to climb. We climbed until the top of that hill became a road, and we took that too. We rode along all the old roads I'd once taken. 1428. 114. 23. We passed the mouths of hollows, the lit windows of houses, doors that opened to let us in. We rode until highways became interstates, until interstates were nothing but mountains. In the distance, some of those mountains had been laid bare, stripped to their bones, made of nothing but grief. But Fannie Ellen still said the old words, the holy ones.

Ginseng. Goldenseal. Yellow root. I said them too, tasted them in my own mouth, tastes as rich as healing, as possibility. "Do you remember?" Fannie Ellen asked. "Do you remember now who you are?"

* * *

Once a friend wrote to me after reading a draft of my novel *Wanting Radiance*. He worried that readers would wonder why late-thirties Miracelle Loving, the main character, hadn't married and settled down yet. He seemed to want a stronger plot, maybe a plan for my character's life. I sat down, trying hard to sketch a plan for Miracelle, but all I came up with were questions. *Why choose riding the roads over a home? Is it because of how highways sound at night? Can strangers fill up your heart more than safety and love?* Those were all questions I asked myself until I was forty-five and chose to share my life with a partner. Questions. Dreams. Journeys. Those are the ways stories have revealed themselves to me. *Narrative arc. Structure. Plot.* Are women's lives always that clear? Mine certainly hasn't been. The journeys have always been challenging, both on the page and along the roads I've traveled.

If I asked Miracelle Loving or any of those women I have imagined whether their journeys have been straightforward, I think they'd say no. Miracelle might describe some night ride on a highway she took on a whim—a whim that led to a two-lane, then to an unmarked gravel road and some juke joint with a broken neon sign, a great place to get just one drink before heading on her way. Who knows what could happen next? That's Miracelle's story, and it was my own, for years and years. Sometimes, I've come to think, my stories have meant that an ending might well come before the middle, followed by another surprising turn in the road. The opening might end up being on the last page, just as the lights to the last bar come on. *Beginning. Middle. End.* What paths do women's stories take along those arduous journeys toward becoming themselves?

* * *

I still wait for the eastern Kentucky earth to tell me something. I grieve for land that no longer exists, for mountains razed by highways, highways slashing through the memory of wilderness. I grieve for memories and the people long gone. I am gone, too, in a lot of ways. I have chosen a different path than Fannie Ellen wanted for me. I rise up with good daylight, but it's to write the stories of what was and the stories of what might be. I'm a seeker. I drive home to Kentucky again and again, trying to summon the ghosts of all the places that once were. Like Miracelle Loving says as she contemplates the places her journey toward peace has taken her, "I didn't know of what I was more afraid—roads out, or all the roads leading inside." I don't much know either, but I take the next turn, and the one after that.

NOW AND THEN

My Grand Canyon days are time seen through a thick glass jar held up to the sun. Forty years is a narrow corridor of time, considering the over ten thousand years of the canyon's history, the four thousand years of Native American habitation of the canyon and its environs, the archaic pictographs and petroglyphs on the canyon's rock walls far older than that. I was a twenty-something seeker. I wanted poetry and God, visions and truths, in whatever order they came to me. It was 1982, and I'd married, unmarried, worked jobs. I'd loved, cut all my ties. I'd traveled to the canyon to work for Fred Harvey's tourism industry to earn a living and see the world, but I also believed I'd taken a path toward pure light. Anything was better than my own chaotic world.

These many years later, I'm outside at night in my neighborhood, looking at streetlights burned out since a recent storm. Summer 2023, and I'm living on the outskirts of Baltimore, and I stand listening to low-flying planes, sirens, the barking of dogs. The night is a slow cooker, a wait-and-see. Early July has meant some of the hottest days on record across the globe, and the hot dark sticks to my skin. That has been true for years now—a near decade of simmering darkness, of worldwide pandemic, climate crisis, and all the manifestations of hate, pure and simple. But I tell myself there will be no slouching towards Bethlehem, not quite yet. If I try to remember, surely there will be a memory canyon filled with light, and that will do some good. Surely mercy will bring stillness to the face of the deep. Magic, that sparkle and shine, can exist even now. There will be words to summon happenstance, if not possibility. Surely the world can be new again, can be good again, amen.

My second winter as an employee at the Grand Canyon, it was dark and cold, with powdery snow on the ground. Each morning, I slip-slid my way through the far reaches of the employee housing parking lot, then up a flight of steps behind the El Tovar Hotel, crimping my toes inside my boots, finding purchase on the icy asphalt. One morning, I was breathing hard after the climb, and I was early, so I found half a joint in my pack when I reached the large back patio. It was midwinter, there were few tourists, and the lights at 5:00 a.m. were half on, half off. I closed my eyes, feeling the icy air freezing my nose hairs.

I'd thought I had the place to myself, but a voice came from the back recesses of the patio. A beautiful man I'd seen a time or two at the El Tovar lounge was perched on one of the wooden deck chairs, his knees in his arms. His long blue-black hair was tied with a red strip of cloth and tucked into his jeans as he rose when I offered him the joint. We said nothing as we gazed across the far reaches of the canyon, the not quite light gathering like mist. Birds floated out of nowhere and dived into the canyon.

He was Hopi, he'd said when I'd tried to talk to him at the lounge. Hopi, Havasupai, Paiute. Those were some of the tribes who worked at the canyon, same as the rest of us did, but going down there? It was off-limits, sacred space, he said as I told him about the trails I'd been taking. Crazy bohana, he called me, like the locals called most of us. We installed ghost tours, put up signs, built hotels. The beautiful Hopi man and I listened to the whoosh of birds and to whatever it was down there in the canyon's bottom, where I hiked all the time and where no Native American would ever set foot.

* * *

No better word for the world these days than *crazy*. We've lived through the reign of misrepresentations, a leader who wept before heaven at the sight of children dead from chemical weapons, all the while planning a great wall to keep everyone but us at bay. It was, he said, merely coincidental that there were nearly nine hundred hate crimes across the US in the ten days following his election. Chaos has festered. As of July, news accounts say, there have been 330 mass shootings (defined as four or more victims) in 2023 so far. On the July 4, 2023, holiday weekend, there were shootings in Maryland, Texas, Louisiana, Pennsylvania, the District of Columbia, Michigan, Minnesota, Indiana, Ohio, California, and New York. Solutions to our love of violence abound. In another news account, a famous celebrity denied that the Holocaust happened, all the while declaring that it *should* have occurred. Six million Jews should have died, she claimed. We'd have been, she said, a much safer world.

* * *

I was a maid at the Bright Angel Lodge, one job on the list of those I'd drifted into since I was sixteen—fast-food worker, convenience store clerk, stenotypist, teletype operator. I'd graduated from community college, and I'd graduated from a four-year liberal arts college, but I had no real idea what I wanted. I devoured Heidegger's "What Are Poets For?" Saint Anselm's riddles about God in "Faith Seeking Understanding" were my maxim: "God is that, the greater than which cannot be conceived." I had a vocation out there, a just cause, and I held on to writing, a life raft, a rope I believed the universe had tossed me. Writing could pick up the broken world and put the pieces back together with gold. But I couldn't quite conceive of What Came Next. I painted walls for a time. I bought multiple notebooks with fancy covers and scribbled in them at lunch and early in the morning. I thought about more school, then began to research jobs at national parks concessionaires in Utah, New Mexico, and Arizona. I stove-cemented the cracked block in my 1967 Dodge Dart and headed west.

My destination was the Grand Canyon, where my summer Fred Harvey contract spilled over into fall. I worked five and sometimes six days and hiked the trails with my time off, but as winter set in, the world got smaller, and dark came early. I spent lots of time with Dave, a carpenter for Harvey Maintenance; he made me vegetarian meals and shared his visionary drugs. Once we did blotter acid and spent all night watching the tiny nuns in *The Sound of Music*. Another night we camped out at Lake Powell and drank the full moon in long swallows.

Other nights I fell asleep with my writing notebook on my mattress on the floor in employee housing. I wrote down lines that began well enough but then skittered away into nothing. *Shine of the moon. Eyes of the ringtail cat.* What I wrote down were dreams, halves of poems, sketches of what I'd seen or overheard or wished. What I wrote down were parts of memories of a son I'd relinquished, lives I'd tried on to fill up the hole inside myself. It would take me years to begin to understand exactly what it was I was mourning as I stared into the dark, when I felt my way across the apartment to the bathroom, peed, and then stood looking at the mirror, seeing nothing but a blank where a self should have been. I was a lost girl, a not-yet-woman. I was nobody I could name, and I liked it that way, even if I wanted to believe that words could change the world.

* * *

Some nights, reading a long litany of facts on my phone lulls me to sleep. As of July 2023, there have been 496 days since the start of the invasion in Ukraine. Over eighteen thousand civilian casualties; over two hundred thousand casualties on all sides; twenty-six thousand casualties among Russian soldiers. Or consider some other kind of warfare, on other species—a recent infographic shows that among plants, amphibians, and corals, 40, 35, and 30 percent of assessed species are considered to be threatened with extinction. Related infographics are available for other threatened or vulnerable species: the Asian elephant, the Amur leopard, the black rhino, the giant anteater, the Bornean elephant, the arctic fox, the sloth, the polar bear, the grass snake, the Malaysian giant turtle, and on and on and on until the words have left my mouth and I once again fall into a fitful sleep in which I dream of nothing but barren earth.

* * *

Hiss of snow falling from boughs near the canyon. Jukebox at the bar at night. Sounds of doors opening and closing up and down the halls of the Bright Angel Lodge. Come midwinter, I'd been made a housekeeping supervisor, which meant opening door after door of the one hundred lodge rooms to check them out for good-enough cleanliness. My step up in the world from maid to supervisor was no promotion; I'd been demoted to the easier-to-finish-on-time position.

Being a maid meant twenty rooms, two large beds, and a shower and tub, and I was slow. I was slower than the high school kid who made the beds without changing the sheets. I was slower than Kenny, the assistant houseman, who dawdled in the stayovers, stealing bottles of cologne for his girlfriend or rings and once a gold watch to pawn in Flagstaff. I was way slower than the housekeeping staff, a group of Havasupai who'd been working at the Bright Angel for generation unto generation.

Julia Polyquiva, head housekeeper, was a plump-cheeked woman in her midforties who laughed at much of what I said and sniffed my breath on occasion to see if I'd snuck a drink of Kahlua in a stayover. Faustine, head houseman, whistled through the gap in his front teeth as he heaped his carts with stripped linens and said, "Yeah, yeah," in an upbeat voice as I asked him when the laundered towels were due. Mary, most senior of the maids, cleaned her rooms with speed and efficiency and left wadded-up paper towels under all her beds, just to see if I was really looking. Havasupai identical twins were wonders with getting their rooms done, quick, quick, but they had taken to removing the Being Serviced signs from the door handles of the rooms where they were working. I went from room to room looking for them, opening and shutting door after door, but found only a sprinkling of cigarette ash in the dresser drawers, single hairs on new but unopened bars of soap.

I was twenty-something, one hundred and five pounds, and heavy with unnamed grief. I'd come to the Grand Canyon for money and adventure, but I also wanted magic. I wanted healing. I wanted to be healed, but the closest I'd come was a childhood baptism I no longer believed in and, more recently, peyote sickness as I walked Brushy Creek back in Kentucky and saw stray branches turn into serpents. While I walked the Bright Angel inspecting rooms, I imagined healing arriving in my life in some unexpected form. Maybe Faustine's "Yeah, yeah" would turn into words I could see, and the words would turn into sage and a blessing I could inhale, or maybe the wadded-up papers underneath the beds in Mary's rooms were inscribed with petroglyphs I could translate for the here and now. I told myself they knew magic.

Leetha Talesyusia, not quite thirty, looked forty with her years of chain-smoking and her big, sad eyes. Leetha was a master cleaner, surpassed only by her daughter, Tina. Leetha and Tina shared rooms, with one doing the beds while the other did the bath and shower before they met in the middle for furniture polishing and vacuuming. Leetha, a single mother, started at Bright Angel the year after she had Tina, who was now fifteen and pregnant, on the road to being a single mother herself.

In the halls of the Bright Angel, I told myself we exchanged understanding looks about pregnancy and all that came after. I drew pictures of that understanding, hallucinatory ballpoint-pen drawings of women, umbilical cord–like threads connecting them. I wrote lines about what I wanted to talk with Tina about: "Legs

spreading open / the world come open / the child without a name."
I imagined myself a teacher of young Native mothers, a mentor
for a whole legion of hurt women, our heads bent over our writer's notebooks. "Tell your stories," I'd say to them, and I imagined
their stories and mine marching forward onto page after page. The
truth was that the afterbirth Tina had expelled was the same as the
afterbirth I'd expelled, and it hurt just as much, holding nothing in
our arms, for both of us, but in the halls of the Bright Angel, Tina
and I never spoke a word to each other.

* * *

The mystery of trails, the fascination of highways. I-40 West. I-70.
Road out of the Grand Canyon toward Flagstaff. AZ 64 to the Super-
stition Mountains, where my hair sparked with lightning. Highway
89 to Lake Powell and a dive from a cliff as I held my breath and
wondered if I'd make it. Black Canyon Freeway to Phoenix, the
radio cranked up loud to *The Beatles*, "Back in the USSR." A mining
town on Highway 66, my pockets full of pottery shards I'd much
later give to the son who lived in Arizona, that son I met years
after relinquishing him at birth. Route 180 to Flagstaff, summer
and winter, once with snow piled high and electric lines waving in
the moonlight, alive with mescaline. Bright Angel Trail. Hermit.
Thunder River. South Rim to North, North to South. Once, climbing
back up the Bright Angel before dawn, I took a switchback and came
upon a bighorn who vanished just as the sun began to rise. Trails
and highways, roads and paths leading nowhere, and occasionally
a somewhere you hold on to.

* * *

Of the trails I hiked back then, the Kaibab was the most difficult.
If I look up that trail now on a site for the park, this is what I find:

"Steep, no water, little shade. Water available seasonally at the trail-head. Upper portion of the trail may be extremely icy in winter or early spring." My plan was to hike down, scoop up some pieces of copper at the deserted mine, say a prayer: "Now I lay me down to sleep," or "Star bright, star light." Crazy bohana me, striding down the steep, snow-covered Kaibab at four o'clock with the sun on its way down.

It got dark and almost cold, fast. Howls and yips crescendoed in the distance, so I sussed out the shack right away. Not a shack, really, but a structure made of boards with a tin roof, no more than three feet high, an old miner's lean-to. I rolled out my sleeping bag and crawled in with my boots and my flashlight and my pack and my water bottle. I huddled up and listened to the coyotes, lay in the dark clicking the flashlight on, off, on, off. I swung the flashlight's beam here, there, then to the corner of the lean-to, where I saw lizards and their skinny tails. The bone-scraped white teeth of bigger things. I sank into a restless sleep, then woke again, hearing it. *Scrape and scratch. Scratch and skittle.* In my memory, I heard full-out nails on tin. Somersaults and pirouettes. Guffaws. I sat up, flashlight in hand. I scooted close to the six-inch opening in the board side of the lean-to. I flicked an arc of flashlight across an expanse of desert. Nothing. I lay down again, wide awake, mind spinning. What was out there? Restless sleep tickled my insides. I tossed and turned. I dreamed. I wandered.

I wandered back east and saw myself, where I'd be again in a year, two years. Girl-me, a little older, her legs still strong from hiking all the miles, her plans still untethered, her grief still intact. What did I want to do with who I was? What was I capable of doing with who I'd been? Out in the dark, whatever it was drummed again on the metal roof, and this time I lay still and let the sounds wash over me. I imagined faces out there in the dark. I saw the face of Leetha Talesyusia. The face of her daughter, Tina. The face of Tina's unborn baby, my own baby.

I wanted to meet the spirits that live in the Grand Canyon, wanted the pictographs I'd seen to translate themselves into visions, wanted those visions to come alive, guide my hands. The scratching on tin started and stopped, and I wanted whatever it was to have a name. I sat up, swung my flashlight's beam all around, but saw nothing. The sounds were bats. They were memories. The sounds morphed into tiny words taking flight into the night, but the minute I clicked on the flashlight, there was nothing but silence.

* * *

I sit in bed sipping white wine and reading a *New Yorker* essay. Thursday, April 14, 2017. The first-ever combat dropping of a massive bomb, technically called GBU-43/B, Massive Ordnance Air Blast, known in military circles as the "mother of all bombs" because of its size and power. The MOAB is thirty feet long, has a 40.5-inch diameter, and weighs 21,717 pounds, with a warhead weighing in at 18,739 pounds. It has a blast yield of eleven tons and a blast radius of one mile, demolishing everything within that one square mile. "The earth felt like a boat in a storm," Mohammed Shahzadah told the *Guardian* after the detonation of the MOAB in Afghanistan. "It felt like the heavens were falling." Such a world horrifies me. That world is a clock. Another bomb waiting to explode. Time ticks on. I sit in bed sipping my wine, and the world is out there, and I am not it. How do we resist a dark world? With art? Anger? How about prayers? Or with, as the self-help manuals say, fearless personal inventory? What does it mean to look inside a heart, deep into its chambers, its vessels, its passageways that carry the blood back, forth, back again?

* * *

One afternoon as I was inspecting the last of the Bright Angel rooms, I stood in the lamplight near the dresser and checked to see if I looked as wrung out as I felt. I'd stayed out till 2:00 a.m. drinking whiskey shots and throwing darts with the beautiful Hopi man. He hit the bullseye on the dartboard every single time, and I bought rounds. Some friends of his came in, two Havasupai girls I'd seen around, and the three of them huddled by the bar, glancing at me, and I was ashamed in some unspecified way, like that time I was lost on the streets in Flagstaff and went up onto the porch of the local Bureau of Indian Affairs. Another crazy bohana who had no idea where she was.

What did I want from that Hopi guy anyway? A holy man to look me in the eyes and tell me what I'd forgotten or never known in the first place? The truth was, I'd come all this way west to find myself. I was looking for a miracle, and now what? A sweat lodge? Some good peyote from the desert? The truth was deeper than skin, deeper than blood. I wanted a truth more ancient than any race, something beneath my skin, inside my bones.

I wiped fingerprints from the mirror in the Bright Angel room, opened the dresser drawers to make sure no one had left anything behind. They had. One of the drawers was full of recruitment flyers for the Ku Klux Klan. Slogans about race and purity with racist, cartoonish drawings. I emptied the drawer and took everything back to the housekeeping office, where Julia Polyquiva put the flyers in her desk and locked it, and we never spoke of it again.

* * *

Forty years since then. A million. No time at all, but I can easily see myself that last canyon day, how I cleaned out my closet, deciding what to take, what to leave behind. I threw away sheet sets, sweaters, books. I left behind my carpenter lover with a kiss and a promise I never kept. As I drove away, I left a trail of debris behind me, all the unexplored love and unknown canyons of my heart tossed out the windows of my car, a life I no longer wanted on the way to the next life and the one after that. A trail of black smoke coughed out the tailpipe of my Dodge Dart. Ahead of me? I'd seen it all, so I thought. Drug dreams. Deserts. I'd listened to unknown tongues. And there'd been that untidy vision that night at the bottom of the canyon near a deserted copper mine. Now I was going to write something or other and somehow change the world.

* * *

I remember the moment I opened a dresser drawer at the Bright Angel to find garish orange and purple and green flyers. I remember some of the words: blood, honor, and purity. The world now has changed, and it has not changed at all. Ours is an age of misinformation, cruelties, and power plays. Hatred abounds. Racism, misogyny, sexism, classism, elitism, an unending list. Floods. Hurricanes. Fires. All are the texts and subtexts of this age of ours.

My own truth is the only thing I have with which to confront this world, and I am as much an uncertain seeker as I ever was. I lie at night with my phone, flicking on the news feed, scrolling past yesterday's stories. My heart beats faster, frightened and uncertain of what, exactly, the power of any one heart is in this huge, vulnerable world. Other nights, I lie awake listening to words in the dark. They whiz and buzz and titter. *Catch me if you can.* The words flash light, and I reach my hands out, waiting. If I'm lucky, they land on my palms, settling for just a little while. I study them, hoping to understand their shape and definition. *Love. Anger. Kindness.* I hold these words in my mouth, tasting them, looking for all the possibilities, for any one meaning, some true power.

AND THEN THE HOLY RIVER

I told myself that if I knelt by the Ganges, the river of forgiveness, then all would be well. If I scooped up the river's holy waters, an absolution, surely I would find poems again. I had told myself this for all the days we lingered in Varanasi, but we had not yet stood beside the Ganges. I had lit incense at the temples of gods whose names I didn't know. We had sipped hot tea to make our bodies sweat, cooling ourselves in the midday heat. I told myself again that all would be well as I stood on a rooftop, relishing Varanasi's cooler night air. In my pockets were pebbles, and I was tossing them into the street. *Mystery. Light. Hunger.* With each pebble, a word. "What are you doing?" you asked. We'd been traveling for over a year, had been together for two years before that, but I still struggled to tell you about the things I loved. *Moment. Books. Memory.* "Thinking poems," I said at last. "Thinking beauty."

You took a pebble and tossed it. "Is poetry always beautiful?" you asked. The question wandered back from the edge of the rooftop, settled inside me, an ache. That afternoon, I'd sat with my notebook near the market, making a list of words. *Teeming world. Red bindi like an eye.* Then I'd seen the man near the wall, in what passed as shade. He sat beside a mound of dirt and rocks, holding an umbrella over his head against the fierce sun. I'd imagined a poem like ice on his neck, the world made cool with imagining as he broke stones into gravel in the heat.

* * *

Once upon a time, poems flew by themselves. They were three days of black beauties from Peace Park. They were lost in the words on bathroom stall doors. They were found on the backs of napkins, inside matchbooks. They were packed into bags that traveled to Arizona, to New Mexico. They grew near highways, beside roads headed back east. They took themselves seriously in classrooms at a big, fine school. They learned names for themselves. *Ghazal. Pantoum. Cinquain.* They reached inside hearts that refused to open. They became journeys. The woman alone in a diner. The woman beside the man on a bus. The poems were deserts and mountains and caves. Poems were a man's bare feet near a fire and its cooking pots. Poems were the city of Varanasi.

* * *

We got to Varanasi, the city of light, via school bus, riding rooftop with a press of bodies and a heap of metal pipes. The bus careened down hills, took curves so fast I slid onto the girl lying sick beside a crate of chickens. The sun, yellow and mean, bore down as we rode through villages, all of us ducking under the wires that sagged across the roads. "God is great," someone called as I vomited from the edge of the bus into the white-hot day. They all sang, and you sang too, though neither of us necessarily believed in God. You came from tidy Eucharists and real wine in silver cups, while I came from praise-the-Lord preachers and the laying on of hands. I'd followed you to Varanasi, city of heat and devotion, a pilgrimage I was trying to understand.

The center of Varanasi was where your old friend A. lived. A. was a scholar, devoted to the study of Goswami Tulsidas, the great Hindu poet who had once lived by the banks of the Ganges. We were invited to crash for two days with A. until we got our bearings. Our room was small—a desk, a low bench, a window, and on its wide sill a many-armed god and a mound of red powder glowing in the fierce sun. "Will you be comfortable here?" A. asked me. He showed us a place for our packs and sleeping bags behind a folding screen in a corner.

I'd met friends of yours from England and France, Greece and Australia. In France there'd been the family who owned a vineyard, their son an old buddy of yours from once upon a time in an Israeli kibbutz. We'd stayed a month in Greece with a wild-haired woman named Jodi, sleeping on the rooftop of an apartment on a winding brick street in Chania. In Australia, there was Steve, a surfer who rode the waves near Botany Bay. When I was with your friends, I was quiet, telling myself I was storing up truths for later. On my notebook's cover was an Anne Sexton quote: "Put your ear down close to your soul and listen hard."

Here we were, the two of you talking about the years since Virginia. You'd been saving to travel, and A. was writing about the difference in poems, west and east. You wanted roads ahead, you said, and not roads inside the pages of books. You sat on the floor, legs crossed, sipping pinkish tea, then mentioned that I wrote poems, as if you'd remembered. A. touched the red mound of powder. "Tell me what a poem is," he asked, placing a finger to my forehead.

* * *

My first poems were moments. A box fan blowing warm air across the living room. My mother on the couch, my father in his chair, me in the space between, learning to read the sadness of their faces. Later, their muffled voices from the other side of a wall. The hiss of arguing. A drawer sliding open. The rearrangement of bodies, the give of the mattress, in, out, in, out. "I love you like no other woman," a voice said, and then there was silence.

Poems traveled behind the Plymouth Duster the first boy drove, drifted into the rolled-down windows as we parked in a thicket of trees beside Highway 60 going west. The poems folded themselves small inside my pockets when I ran away from home. One poem wrote itself in that apartment in St. Louis while a boy held a knife to my throat and told me he wanted me. *Jim. Michael. Wayne. Steve.*

Poems were made of boys, one and two and so on, until there were men. *Donny. Tom. Otis.* Slack-skinned men smelling of beer and roadsides and motel rooms where I wrote poems in the backs of Bibles.

There was the woman who wove shawls who said that my aura was blue as she made love to me. There was the woman with sad eyes I kissed and kissed in a country music bar. A man who cried when we both came as we lay in the heat of his apartment, the rim of the canyon outside piling up with snow. The poems were wind blowing against a bell hanging from the eaves of a house I left, some lover watching out the window as I drove away.

* * *

You became my lover because of a volcano . . . the main attraction at Green Gardens, a greenhouse next to Highway 29 North in central Virginia. I was a student, studying in a master of fine arts program. I needed work, and so I was hired to help haul and dig and plant. The volcano was forty feet high, a dormant mound of dirt and rocks circled with plastic tubing that released water to simulate lava. You were kneeling at its base on that muggy August day we met. You were digging up irises to separate and plant. I remember studying the planes of your sunburned cheeks, the flat tips of fingers that would soon be inside my body.

In the distance was a busy highway, all the cars. I waited as you interrupted the rhythm of spade and soil. I don't remember you asking my name, looking at me. You were working here, you said, until you were ready to head east. What about me? I didn't answer. I wanted the volcano to spew cool water right then. I wanted us to stand in its shower, dissolving the day's heat. "Where east?" I asked. I remember the dry feel of the dirt as I reached my hands in, picked up the first cluster of irises.

* * *

The marketplace was heavy with the scents of curries, listless with Varanasi's premonsoon air. I touched the gold bindi on an elephant's trunk. Lord Ganesha, a toothless woman said as she laid garlands of jasmine around his enormous head. *Ganesha.* God of scribes and writers. We were in a guesthouse by then. Afternoons, the table where we ate was hot to the touch, and afterward we napped for hours in the blazing heat. Evenings, we wandered in streets crowded with everyone too restless to sleep in the heat, with music and the angry eyes of stray dogs. Night. We got up every few hours to stand under a shower's warm water, slept naked as a fan dried us cool, leaving our sheets brown from the waters of the Ganges.

Once, a few hours before dawn, I left you sleeping. On the balcony, I heard calls to prayer from the distant muezzin. In the street below, a legless man rolled by on a platform. A woman wailed as she walked by carrying a bundle of straw on her back. The jangle of a bell on a bicycle. Coughing from a man on a balcony across the way, the toss of water from his metal pitcher into the street. The world was a moan, an awake sigh, the night's resistance to heat. I told the day to wait. Soon I would go back inside and lie down a little longer, listening to your breath rise and fall.

* * *

In the weeks after we met, I worked in the greenhouse, then hurried to workshop, where we dissected our poems, line by line by line. I wanted to hold my poems up, let light show through the pages. What was the heart of the words I'd written? *Longing* was an only adequate word, but it was as close as I could get. In the apartment where you lived, the living room was empty except for a dining table and an enormous plastic blow-up of Godzilla. I listened to the echo of your footsteps as you fetched a glass of water, then came back to bed. I held those echoes between my fingers, then let them go.

* * *

We purified our water with iodine, drank it warm from the bottle while we walked and walked. In the streets of Varanasi, we passed straw huts where voices urged us to drink, drink, fifty paise for a metal cup of water poured cool and impure into our open hands. On a day trip to a holy site, vendors pressed chilled bottles of Limca cola against our arms as we waited for the bus in the hot sun, the only shadows from the packed lines of people, people. Palms patted chapati thin beside small fires, and large, gray pigs rooted in the trash in a lot where the bus stopped. Curries churned in our guts as we licked our fingers clean. A vendor with a case full of picks and tiny awls promised to clean our ears and tell our fortunes. In an alleyway, a temple with an open doorway and dancers with shorn heads. A priestess chanting. *Om Namah Shivaya.* Our days were orange, brown, red, blue, an impasse of color, no color a clue to what this city was, what it meant.

* * *

Those first months in Virginia, knowing you had refrains: *You were here just for a little while. You were here just until you had the money. You were staying only until.* Until then, you were here, and I was here, and so we spent evenings at your apartment sipping wine and petting a cat named Velcro. That night in your room, I eyed the piles of socks and pants and shirts, the open drawers of a chest. There was a story. Once, you said, someone broke into the house where you were living with some friends. No one could tell what had been taken from your room because of the disarray. I wondered if I should laugh.

You unbuttoned me, and I unbuttoned you. I'd followed the script a hundred times over the years, reaching across space to someone I hardly knew. What I did know: your silence, your self-containment as you worked the nine-hour greenhouse days.

Your no-small-talk ways. Your tall reach in the sun as you bent, shoveled, bent. In your eyes, a hint of all the countries I'd never seen, the oceans, the faraway lures. I memorized the little beads of sweat that had dried in the hairs under your arms.

There was the curtainless window and the dull shine of street-light. The scratch of a cat's claws at the door. All the men before: their bodies houses I would enter, making sure that I was a good guest, that I proffered just the right gifts of hands and mouth. You lay on your side, and I faced you, waiting beside a chasm, this first foray of body into body. There was the chiaroscuro of arms and legs, a woman posing on the verge of opening herself. I imagined shutting open drawers, folding stray socks, touching you precisely here and there, where surely all the truest words lay.

* * *

Our Varanasi room was cheap and good, a stifling box. A low bed sat on blocks, the walls smoky and streaked with what could have been blood. I imagined an arm, a spurt from the tip of a heroin-filled needle. Voices bartered for drugs and everything else all day long. *Change money. Buy passport.* The streets were never still. A family sleeping on cots in the street began to wake up. A girl took up an enormous bundle of laundry and carried it atop her head. A woman knelt, blowing fire alive under a burner to make morning tea. Coughs, shouts, echoes of prayer from the ghats down by the Ganges. That is where we could go to watch the waters move by in this city of cities. I hadn't written a poem in months, and I held the word *holy* in my mouth, waiting for it to come alive.

* * *

I told myself we were poems translated from our own private lan-guages. You clipped vines precisely at the signature leaves. I filled up notebooks with phrases I'd overhead and with drawings of hands. You potted plants and set them out row after row, inside greenhouses smelling like chemicals that could burn the skin. I held my hands out to the sky, waiting for words to fill them up. You watered each hanging pot to the count of ten. I gave you a book about memory and inscribed it with these words: "The worlds of poetry and perennials can meet." You sat eating sharp cheddar sandwiches for lunch week after week after week and would not meet my eyes. I wrote papers about Virginia Woolf. About Mrs. Ramsay, who had died very suddenly during the night. About D. H. Lawrence and Quetzalcoatl. I wrote poems I wanted more than you, and sometimes you read them. You planted gardens that were gold and blue and brilliant red, and you said, "This. *This.*" I dreamed my words grew wings and flew into the pages of books. You came to me in the night, and I came to you in the night, but soon the rooms we found were empty.

* * *

The sixteenth-century saint and poet Goswami Tulsidas woke before sunrise to sit on a balcony overlooking the Ganges. He sipped his sweet tea. Tulsidas didn't know that he would be a famous poet or that he would compose epics delivered directly into the hands of the gods. He didn't yet know that he would swim along the banks of the river in search of Ratnavali, his wife, who had left him, not because he was too much a poet but because he was not poet enough. He had not yet filled himself with language. Ratnavali swept her arms across the expanse of the river, gestured toward the roofs and cooking pots, the temples and alleyways and streets, the marketplaces and the stalls. "You want to write?" she said. "Write this."

* * *

In Varanasi, poetry was a child in an alleyway, all her fingers missing, her hands held out. *Rupee. Rupee.* And you, striding ahead, hoarding coins for all our miles to come. That moment was the start of a poem. "In Varanasi a girl / begs in an alleyway, hungry for coins / while the woman follows the man / who does not know how to translate / a word for need." Poems, a braille I tried and failed to translate. Poems conjured the memory of heat.

* * *

That first Virginia summer passed into winter, and the greenhouse filled with brilliant red poinsettias. You were just as happy if no one knew we were more than friends. Spring was on the clock, tick, tick, and you were leaving by then. *Bali. Thailand. India.* I followed you on maps, dreaming. I trailed after you to parties where your friends shared stories of travels of their own. Your friend Wendy had lived in the city of Calcutta, where she strung beads to make bracelets to sell, sold herself to buy heroin for the man she called her black angel. Marijo and Kevin had traveled to Vietnam to find work in the refugee camps, and Evie had lived in a cave in Greece, on Santorini. And you, they asked as an Elvis Costello song climbed out of the boom box and set them all dancing. "Me," I said. "I try to write poems." That word, *poems*, melted in the steamy heat by the radiator, where you danced with Wendy, your hands on your hips, your eyes shining with the stories you drank in like they were rich, red wine.

Spring came, and you didn't leave for India, and this cost us both. We sat in your 1963 Plymouth Valiant. The windows were rolled down against the heat, and the day was humid and still. I saw myself looking at your blond hair, wanting to run my fingers through it, but I leaned against the open window, studied your ruddy complexion, your one longer tooth, the fine hairs on your arms.

You were in love with buses, with trains and planes that took all night to reach their destination. You were a young man in a safari hat. A lone traveler beside a highway, thumb out for the next ride. The truth was that you loved the India you'd never seen more than you loved me. The truth was that I wanted the idea of love more than I wanted you. I wanted poems that were a distillation of the love that had eluded me. Poems about the family I'd never been able to count on, about the exact way light looked shining down on a pond at night where lovers swam, neither of them us. The argument we were having circled and dived in the air, a blackbird, a bat, a prehistoric being. Surely, I believed, if I held on long enough, I would find the right words.

* * *

Call it a poem. Call it the heat of a late summer night in Varanasi, the city of wild dogs and rabid monkeys sitting on the walls of abandoned palaces. Call it the shape of your mouth as you laughed in that crowded marketplace where we drank bang lassis and watched a sadhu in a loincloth ringing a bell, his eyes blessed with infinity. Call it a story or a song or a chant to summon memory. Call it a photograph you took as I parted that sea of holy cows by holding up my hand. Call it the candles I lit in the monastery and the coins I dropped in the hands of monks. Call it the empty pages of that notebook I carried for month after month, before India, after India, all the lines I meant to fill but never did because there were no words. Or call it this. How once in Varanasi you bought me a rambutan. All the way from the South, the vendor said, nodding with his betel-nut-red smile as he laid the fruit in my palm. I took hold of the soft spikes with my teeth, pulled back the skin, and bit into a sweetness I'd never forget.

* * *

Call the poem this. Call it July. The greenhouses in Virginia sweltering, the long plastic tunnels fecund. The starts of the fall mums were wilting in their pots, and you needed, you said, to tend to them, to water them. You were needed the most then, in the summer's greenhouse heat, you said as you dropped me off early at the door of the clinic where I'd scheduled the procedure before noon. The pregnancy had been inside me for eleven weeks, a secret only you and I knew. I held the secret in the curve of my belly, and you held it in the way your arm draped over my shoulders like it didn't know where to rest.

For ten weeks we had sat in the car, sat in diners, sat in your cluttered room and fought about ways to bring the secret to light, ways to let the secret go. Pregnancy was a termination of your travel plans east, my plans for all the poems. Abortion was a termination, a quick scrape to the womb, the pamphlets said. Ten weeks. Eleven weeks. Most people, the intake person at the clinic said on the phone, want to take care of these things as quickly as possible. Eleven weeks and four days, and I harbored a secret in the fecund red inside myself.

The night after the abortion, I'd get up to pee and find myself sitting on the toilet, studying the radiator, listening to its steam. You'd bought us shrimp and vegetables for supper; we'd sat beside the food, a wake of sorts, and you'd begun to cry, big, silent heaves of your shoulders as you looked at me. Then I'd felt nothing at all, neither for you nor for the pregnancy nor for the flatness I felt inside my belly. As I sat beside the radiator listening to the house sleep, the world shifted into grief and a rage I'd had all my life, and I fell inside its blackness. When I woke, you were standing over me where I lay on the bathroom floor. "Tell me you'll be all right," you said. "*Tell me you'll be all right.*" But that was something I'd never be able to do.

Twelve weeks. I put on the paper gown, lay down on a table, propped my legs up in the stirrups, looked at the doctor's face, and asked him if we could wait, wait just one minute longer. Then his hands were inside me, inserting a tube that sucked the thing out. The thing, the secret, the accident, the wish. "Abortion," the definition reads, "to bring to premature end because of a problem or fault."

I'd imagined it for twelve weeks, the secret rushing out of my womb.

I told myself it would be like warm water from between my legs. It would be moistness from an underground cavern, a hidden chamber, a refuge. It would be easy. It would be quick. It would be over, over. It would come out of me, and I would capture it later like a poem. It was a secret released into the air, a mourning I would try to release, but I breathed it back in, and I couldn't let go of it after, as hard as I tried.

* * *

In time I will summon words to describe those Varanasi days—alleyways, stalls, frangipani blossoms at the altars of the dead. I will write poems and stories about why I went there, will open a box of photographs, and the memory of heat will rise against my face. Some nights I will dream of maps and a tangle of roads, buses, and the faces of strangers. In one dream, you will meet me on a dead-end street at night, where we speak to each other again after many years of silence. In another dream, you will show me a garden so beautiful it makes me weep. In time I will hold the words I least understand in my mouth until I taste them. *Ganges, Holy River.* After so many years, if I summon enough words, can I make a poem that both remembers and forgets?

* * *

The holy river called Sindhu. It descended once from a glacier, become vast tributaries, become an epic, given the name of kings and queens. *Ganga. Mother of Forgiveness.* I still feel the mud between my toes as I waded into that river called Ganges. You were behind me with your camera, photographing the women in their saris, waist deep and bathing. Ibis winged up toward a sun that blinded me through my spread fingers. Old man in the bow of a shikara, hookah and fragrant smoke. Plump body of a dead man floating past, his face down in the holy waters. I waded farther into the sacred river, its stagnant waters covering my thighs. I took a handful of dust gathered from the ghat where you were standing. I scattered it over the waters like the remains of the dead.

SUPPLICATION

1.

I still hear the drip of night humidity as it fell from the tamarind tree under which we'd camped. I see sunlight climbing over the horizon as I woke each morning, taste the bitter salt in my throat as I dived in, bathing in the sea's warm waters. I see the burnt red of the trail I climbed to a temple. Along the trail, one creature had devoured another, leaving gray fur, the broken spines of feathers. I picked up a pelvic bone and strung it on red thread to wear around my neck. Long after, it reminded me of that place of arroyos and azure sea. I still remember how the air smelled of cedar and heat, like holy incense.

Since I was eighteen, I'd been followed by a black dog, that despairing ghost. I'd moved from town to town, from lover to lover. For two years I'd traveled with Paul, lover turned friend, friend I trusted no more than I trusted anyone else in my life. We hitched and rode buses and stowed away from Ireland to England, from England to Yugoslavia, from Yugoslavia to Greece, from Greece north into Asia. As we traveled, I felt the thing inside me rear its head. As we traveled, the black dog nipped and howled. It made me look inside its open mouth and name what I saw.

2.

The tiny island north of Crete was Dia, uninhabited, seven miles from Heraklion. We'd been staying with Jodi, a friend of Paul's from Virginia who lived in Crete, where she was a teacher of English and art. Now the three of us laid out our sleeping bags on the beach as dark settled. There were a million clear stars and in the distance a bonfire and laughter. Down by the water, another boat, and fishermen drinking retsina. "Sit with us," they said, their black eyes laughing. There was wine and there were stories. Tales of other tiny islands where they'd been born, of catching octopuses and swordfish so silver they shone in the moonlight. Stories of diving down so far the world had no sound. Even now, two of them were deaf, and they gestured at Jodi as she argued with them in her fluent Greek. Why, they wanted to know, did she have no husband, and why was she living in Crete, so far from any home? More bottles opened by themselves, the retsina tasting as fresh as the piney boughs of trees. Then the fishermen smashed shells against the rocks and roasted the tender flesh of conch for a feast while Jodi and I danced. Her green eyes were alive as she held the edges of her skirt and circled the fire.

My dream that night was laced with wine and the sea. I dreamed that a beautiful young man walked out of the waves, touched the top of my head. "I forgive you," he said. "I forgive you." The words drummed in my chest. The world was still asleep; Jodi, Paul, sleeping, the sun a dull, not-risen red. The fishermen's boat rocked out from the shore, and I pulled on my clothes. There was a trail behind the tents, and I took it, my bare feet finding purchase in the cool, sandy soil. My soles were tough from months of hiking, hitchhiking, weeks of walking barefoot on the stone streets of Chania, but small sharp rocks bit into my toes as I climbed. The path, Jodi had said, led to the ruins of a temple, and the island had been created by Zeus when he blew lightning into the sea, making a monster that he later made into the islands of Paximadi, and this one, Dia.

In Santorini, I'd lit a candle in some family cemetery right before a storm. In Chania, I'd lit a candle in a chapel at Chrysopigi Monastery, the Women's Convent. And there had been other candles—in a great cathedral in London. A shrine to the Holy Mother on the coast of Ireland. At a roadside shrine near Beograd where the bus stopped for hours one afternoon. This path felt like the desert to my feet. I took in its distances of sand and desolation, then climbed to the top of a large, toppled stone. I looked down on the blue, blue sea and a sky now threaded with blood-colored clouds. Underneath my foot, a shape I prodded with my toes. Feathers. A scrap of gray fur. A bone. I scooped it up, brushing the red dirt from the curves of a pelvic bone smaller than my palm.

All the candles I'd lit had been for memory. They'd been for grief and its demise. And now this dream, of a young man. My son, the one I'd surrendered at birth. The lost boy, living his life out there with a family I'd never met. Adopted out, they called it, and that lent images of hands coming down from the heavens, placing this body here, that body there. My body was here seeking solace on an island created by gods powerful enough to breathe lightning into the sea. And his body, my son's body, was one I'd never seen. I closed my eyes and summoned the beautiful young man as he walked up from the waters, as he reached for me. I blew against the pelvic bone, sending dust like a wish into the hot sun, the ancient sea.

3.

I have always been in love with deserts and oceans, their scents of cedar and salt, their ambience of saints. Saints walking on water. Saints walking mile upon mile as heat rises in waves. They see the world coming open, roiling inside with gods. Baal. Jesus. Abraxas. Vashti. Or maybe oceans and deserts are not about gods at all. Try to find the beginning of the horizon on an early morning by the sea. Or hold your hands out and let dust, red and sparkling with mica, settle there. Winds touch your palms, and soon they are empty, full of nothing.

4.

Saturday nights there was Frank Sinatra and "Some Enchanted Evening" from the transistor radio my mother kept on the medicine cabinet in the bathroom. George Jones crooned from the garage where my father kept his ham radio and his slides of Seoul speakeasies from the Korean War. I knew my parents didn't love each other, and my escape from their emptiness was saints. *Catherine of Siena. Christina the Astonishing.* I loved their slender bodies, their miracles. They lived on rose petals and air.

On Sunday mornings, I sat drawing ankhs and peace signs in the back of my Bible and wishing the time would pass. Later in the church there'd be a Communion, grape juice and crackers, but first the text for the day. A saint I didn't know. Anselm. "There is one nature, supreme among all existing things, who alone is self-sufficient in his eternal happiness." Who, my father later wanted to know, is Saint Anselm? Some Catholic hocus pocus?

I studied the lady with her hat and white gloves. Watched my father clip his nails as hymn words began. Stand. Sit. And down the aisle, stained glass, purple and yellow and red. "I must needs go home by way of the cross," the hymn went as I imagined notes sliding under the pews, moving from person to person. God could slide, like music. Underneath a shut closet door. Between the sweaters and suit jackets in boxes at my grandmother's house. Between my parents' quarrel words. In the church aisles, communion trays passed by. Fronds of lilies down front and waved from the overhead fans. At the end of the aisle, an offering table and an inscription: "Do This. Do This in Remembrance of Me." The preacher, offering salvation. *Saved.* I wanted that. Saved like three brand-new pennies in a dresser drawer. That preacher man up front would have angels in his shirt pocket.

I walked past people and pews as organ music rose. I wanted oceans humming, the desert whispering to Jacob while angels climbed ladders to heaven. Another hymn. His cool, damp hand. "I must needs go home by the way of the cross." He leaned in, his ear almost touching my lips as he waited for me to speak.

5.

I am pedaling through the narrow alleyways of Chania, reciting a saint's blessing to myself: "You once took care of sufferers from the plague and were always ready to help others by kind service and fervent prayers. Bless me now." Bike riding is something I have never mastered, but I steady myself along the uneven cobblestone streets crowded with taxis and cars and other bikers to ask my way to the same beach where I've been again and again: "Which way to the water from here?" I am thirsty and hot and anxious. The signs in Greek tell me nothing. Should I turn back to the safety of Jodi's cool patio?

Near the harbor, I park my bike at a shop where I see a woman in the all-black of grandmothers. She steps out of the shade, steam rising from the black shirt, apron, skirt, scarf, her one fist clutching a squirming chicken. Her wrist flicks once, and the chicken lies limp and dead. "Swimming," I say aloud. She shakes her head and says nothing. We tourists strip down to nothing while the grandmother women watch with disapproval and indifference.

On the beach, I shed my shoes and clothes. Without my glasses, the waters are a blue dream, a cool elixir, and I dive, resurface, dive again. I've been warned about sharks and jellyfish, about women swimming distances alone. By this point, I've traveled for months, hitchhiked, found my way through cities alone. Back in the States, my father wanted me to hide a derringer and a Swiss Army knife in my backpack, though where I'd put them now that I'm naked and swimming is beyond me. The swim is nearly a mile across the channel from the harbor's beach to a small rocky point of land consecrated to the Sacred Mother. Along the roads on the mainland, we have seen shrines: metal boxes on skinny wire legs, small glass doors, a candle flickering, a saint staring back.

"Blessed art thou among women, blessed is the fruit of thy womb, Jesus." I pray to Mary as I freestyle, backstroke, the warm salt water sliding along my arms and across my bare breasts, along my kicking legs. I wonder if the woman on the beach boils the chicken until the bones are bare, if she uses the bones to tell lives. In the evenings at my friend's house in Chania, there is a tin-framed mirror in a courtyard, and I study my sunburned face, eyes that have seen whole worlds and will see more. We have plans for Nepal, Thailand, India. I no longer have any predictions for the self that lies ahead. In Chania, Jodi and her friends have taken to calling me Catherine because of my love of the saints, and this name is as good as any other.

When I reach the point of land across the channel, I will walk the last yards up onto smooth, flat stones. I will walk along whitish sand toward the shrine. This shrine is no larger than a child's playhouse, its front glass over an image of Mary, the Mary who sorrowed at her dying son's feet, the Mary who traveled road upon road spreading word of that son's eternal love, her heart empty with grief. A candle is lit each day at this shrine, though I have never seen another soul. I have no matches, and without my silver-framed glasses, I will be able to see nothing but the shapes of things. I will feel my way along the hot sand, lay my hands along the cool, whitewashed shrine, and pray as if I am blind.

6.

Saint Thérèse of Lisieux, the Little Flower. Saint Anselm, lover of the understanding of faith via reason. Saint Lucy, she of clarity, radiance, and light. Saint Nicholas of Myra, the patron saint of travelers. The Virgin of Guadalupe, a medal I wear. I was brought up on what felt like a bitter faith, on sin and impossibility, on visions of a suffering Christ and a woman who knelt, bathing his feet with perfume and drying them with her long hair. Saints have seemed pure to me, full of hunger and grace. I have not understood grace, and yet I have longed for it. I have lit candles in every church, every cathedral I could find in my journeys around the world, and yet I have not truly known how to love. *Love.* What did it know? "Your very flesh shall be a great poem, and have the richest fluency, not only in its words, but in the silent lines of its lips and face," Whitman said. The saints. Their thin hands, the manuscripts they adorned with flakes of gold. For a long while I believed this was as close to God as I could get.

7.

I'm carrying all I own in a pack balanced on my hips as we climb. Nepal. We hike in its mountains all day, dawn to night. We cross gorges via dilapidated swinging bridges. We head toward unbelievable majesty. Peaks. Temples. Utter poverty. We sit beside a hot spring called Tatopani, and I take off my boots to soak my blistered heels. I sip thin soup at a guesthouse where we're staying for the night. The woman who makes the soup pats out chapatis on a stone beside a fire. "Chapatis quick, quick," she says when we ask for dal. Later I see her combing nits from the hair of her child.

Paul's pack is dusty red, and mine is gray. His holds neatly rolled socks and threadbare shirts. Mine holds those things too, but I've tucked in books that make my weight-bearing harder as we climb. A copy of a minor novel by Thomas Hardy called *A Pair of Blue Eyes.* John Fowles's *The Magus.* I leave these books behind like a trail of breadcrumbs in hostels and guesthouses, and now, in Nepal, the main book I have is a copy of *The Road Less Traveled,* the book Paul's sister gave me as a going-away present. It's about emotional, spiritual, and psychological health, but I'm hesitant when it comes to its loose use of words like *balancing* or *responsibility* or *boundaries.*

By the fourth week in Nepal, the boundaries between body and spirit have diminished. This is true because we have grown thinner and thinner. We subsist on chapatis and iodine-purified water. Over a span of weeks, my insides, writhing with giardia and dysentery, empty themselves out into latrines and holes in the ground. But spirit is detaching from body in other ways. We no longer touch at all, except to help each other climb here, descend there. Paul looks at me with detachment as I throw up in a ditch, and I look at him with unspecified rage. The nearly invisible line that keeps us tethered to each other is growing thinner as the weeks pass.

All through London, I was overwhelmed by the streets and the Underground, the first subway I'd ever seen, and I held on tight to him. I held on even tighter in Paris, where we stopped for a few weeks and I knew about enough French to find my way to a toilet or buy an egg-and-cheese crepe from a street vendor. But now as the days and the miles of these mountains and Sherpas and villages without names pass, I'm shedding the need for Paul, or needing something he can't give, or both. I remind myself that he knows the names of flowers, mysterious and Latinate. *Rudbeckia fulgida* Goldsturm. *Cimicifuga racemosa.* I roll my clothes in my pack just the way he does, and I follow behind him up the trail, step for step, but I've begun to resent him in a secret language I can't articulate, in words that come out in thin, angry sentences. "Tell me what this means," I say, as we pause on the trail at mounds of stones and heaps of red grains of wheat. "It's Nepal," he says. As if that explains why we don't know the name for anything we're seeing. "Namaste," we both say when we pass strangers on the trail. We wish each other no peace at all.

We pass Nepalese valleys full of clouds, trees strung with ethereal monkeys, but at night what I scribble in my notebook are all the names I imagine for God. "If anyone does not know," I've written in a margin of my book, "it is either because he has not heard or because he does not believe." I think this is Saint Anselm speaking, but I am not sure. My memory has begun to fail me more the longer we trek, the longer and farther and more precariously we are away from everything we have ever known. At the same time, the high, thin air and the lean, thin lengths of my own two legs have begun to make me think I understand concepts I've never considered. *Supplication. Atonement.* I feel some special knowledge about God and words inside me. There are truths I think only I can know.

One day at a bend in the trail, we see a child standing beside a hut. She is playing with a stick and prodding at dust and rocks, and she looks at us curiously as we stop mid-trail-bend, intent on the quarrel we're having. Paul has just said that writing is a fine enough hobby but not a thing to *do*, certainly not a thing to make a living at. I am not furious just with this thoughtless statement but with the fact that he has never been a man of words. "I can dream in poetry," I say to him, defensive and pathetic. I have no idea how to describe the writing I want so badly, no less how I see the spiritual experience of this journey we are on. I can name God in twelve ways and in ten times and places in history, but I can't name one of the varieties of poppies Paul once planted by the house where we lived. Back in Virginia, we lay in bed together; my body was the shape of his body, and I'd loved how a fine line of sweat would emerge on his upper brow as he worked. Our bodies do not now equal love. The love I once imagined is behind us. Ahead of us. Out of our reach.

We stop near the child and sling down our packs. "Can you just," I am saying, and he is saying, "Why," and I'm saying, "Why not," and then we both quit, all at once, because the child, a little girl, is tugging at his shirttail. They were always tugging at the straps of my pack or the hem of my dress, the children we met in the streets of Kathmandu, the children we'd met in Pokhara, where our trek began. "Penny, penny," they'd say. "School pens," they'd say, holding out their hands, and I'd give them an ink pen from the airport in London that I'd held on to or one torn-out sheet from my notebook.

This child is muttering two words I don't know, over and over, and she's holding her hands together next to her chest and peering down into them, then up at us. I'm already fumbling in the side pocket of my pack, looking for two cents or a nickel, and Paul has his hands on his hips, his mouth still set and his eyes tired from the fight we've had, and all the while a cloud is inching its way up over the edge of the trail. A cloud full of light and dust, a cloud full of rain, though summer is a dry and rainless season in Nepal.

I'll remember the cloud drifting up and over, slipping between us for just a second, making us disappear from each other like we soon would, for good. Then I found them, two dimes I held out, and she held out her little girl hands with their bitten nails. She opened her palms, in them the tiny embryo of a bird.

8.

"Is it by traveling that we prove God exists?" Saint Anselm asked. I have put together my own answers to the question like the pieces of a quilt my grandmother used to make: Trip around the World. The quilt is made of successive journeys of color around the circumference until you reach the center, one solid square of yellow, like a light in the middle of a maze.

My quilt's first journey is red, along the outside—my ancestors on a snaky two-lane in the eastern Kentucky mountains. They are singing: "Shall we gather at the river, the beautiful, the beautiful river." My father's journey is next, in green. Two years in Korea, and afterward he bought my mother a diamond engagement ring from Morocco, wrote her letters from Seoul, which I keep in a box near my writing desk. Their journey together is next, in gray. A flat sky always holding rain, a loveless marriage, a sunlight they never reached. The next trip around the world is blue. Me, sitting between my parents as we rode over Cumberland Gap and stopped at a country store for cheese slices and saltines. And all the journeys after that. Trip upon trip upon trip. Orange and white. Lavender and rose. India. Nepal. Thailand. A back alley in a forgotten street in another unremembered country.

What do we call the passages in a journey? What do we name the spaces between words on a page? The distance between the pencil and the mark it makes? What fills the blank space between prayers unanswered and ones never said? One journey becomes the next; mountains and deserts and oceans become a world that goes on and on.

9.

Histories tell us not to idealize the childhoods of saints. Saint Anselm, born Anselmo di Candia Ginevra in the city of Aosta in 1033, was raised by a noble family. His father, Gundulph, was by birth a Lombard and seems to have been harsh and often violent; his mother, Ermenberga, gave Anselmo careful religious instruction but also shielded him from his father, with whom he had nothing in common but dislike. "Make something of yourself," his father said, and he meant gold coins and properties and a bride who would produce generations. "My name," the father said, "must go on."

Accounts show a dutiful young man who, at fifteen years, longed to become a monk but could not obtain the consent of either his father or the abbot of the local monastery. In 1059, after his mother died and his father's harshness became unbearable, he fled. He was almost twenty-seven years old by then and had only the vaguest plans. He dreamed of a prosperous city in Lombardy or of a prestigious school where he might study, become a scholar. He ended up crossing the Alps via a southern route, down the Val d'Aosta, then westward, by the Mont Cenis Pass, which would have taken him to the valley of the Rhône where his mother's family lived. Histories say that his crossing of the mountains met with "great discomfort and some danger," but that is where we will leave facts aside and enter the realm of faith.

I imagine young Anselmo traveling alone, carrying nothing, his deep pockets full of paper and bottles of ink he will discard on the trails as the days pass. He is thankful that he thought of trading his fancy velvet breeches for a kitchen servant's gear. He is thankful for the wool traveling cloak, the thick trousers. He has never built a campfire, never been as alone or as hungry as he finds himself now.

There has always been someone lighting lamps, opening doors. There has been a voice to goad him on. *This path. That path.* All the paths, usually down the long stone corridors of a house or a church or some great cathedral of God. As he leaves behind everything he has ever known—quills and tomes and mother love—he is both sorry and not. There has always been his mother at morning prayers, and he has resented her often. Someday he will write a prayer to mothers: "Life-bearer, mother of salvation, shrine of goodness and mercy, I reach out to you. You will deign to heal me."

There are woods beside the trail and the night cries of birds, and he is not quite a boy and not quite a man. He is afraid. He sniffs his palms and imagines a scent of roses and remembers his mother's hair. He lays out his cloak in a mossy place and kneels, determined to say his prayers. Mouth dry, throat aching, he has no words. From the trees, the fiery eyes of creatures he has seen only in the margins of illuminated manuscripts. His breath is warm against his folded hands.

His journals ahead will be full of passages about how we present ourselves to God: "Thine eyes are the eyes of Christ; therefore thou mayest not turn thine eyes to gaze on any kind of vanity; for Christ is the Truth, to whom all vanity is entirely opposed." This night, vanity does not even occur to him. His stomach rumbles, a discordant sound in the night's cold wind. He cannot remember what it is that he wanted in the first place. God? Language? A bed of down and a thick slice of bread?

As night falls, shapes begin to shift. Dark becomes the memory of his mother's hair. Prayer escapes from his folded palms, becomes the shadows, and the shadows become himself. He imagines himself a boy again, and like a boy, he confuses everything. Which is faith and which is hunger? Which is God and which is longing? Someday he will write this: "If something that has a beginning and an end is good, then is something that has a beginning but never ceases to exist much better?" Clouds cross the moon.

10.

A thousand years will pass, and Saint Anselm will live forever and ever, a saint. A dozen years, twenty, more, will pass, and I will travel highways, move past more state lines than I can count before I come at last to the house I call my own. Now I am living at the center of the quilt. The yellow square in the middle of a maze. At that center, there is warmth and love. "The journey," a tarot card told me not long ago, "ends here."

My home, on a quiet street outside a busy metropolis, is a home with food and shelter and comfort. I am as far from deserts as I have ever been, yet before we moved there, my partner and I burned sage from New Mexico. My partner. A gentle man of few words, a Monacan from Virginia who believes in the power of the Creator.

We sent smoke from room to room. To the corners, ceiling-ward. I tell myself we chased them all away, the ghosts of times and places that I had long carried with me, in my pockets and on my back and in my heart. No more dreams, I tell myself, of dishes full of the kernels of wheat I once saw as offerings for the dead along the trail I hiked. I dream of birds and the sounds they make as they dive down to the sea. I dream of my son, my mother, my father, my son, my son, and then I wake into a house cleansed by sage. I write by a window looking out on the lovely bare branches of trees. How lucky I am in this vast world to have found a place to come to rest.

Still, some days I send up prayers, and silence comes back. I remind myself of the emptiness of this world, longing for it and despairing. I am humbled by the loneliness at the heart of all and grieved by a face of God I perhaps will never see. Nights, I sleep in a room beyond which streetlights shine. Winds from a thousand miles away rattle the windowpanes. "Listen," I tell myself. "*Listen.*"

STELLA, IN THE UPSTAIRS ROOM

A story passed down to me from my mother's people was about a woman named Stella. During the 1930s, Stella, it was said, lived in an upstairs room at her brother's and never left the house. The historical facts are vague. She was a distant cousin of mine, or a great-aunt, and her sequestered life was in Dwale, Kentucky. Although I have seen no photos of her, I imagine long, copper-colored hair, a braid winding down her back. She loved the garden below her window, its sunflowers and ripe tomatoes. I think of her alone in her room with bisque-faced dolls for whom she crocheted dresses and the fine handiwork she might have done—pillowcases with initials and roses. I do know that she never married, a thing summed up both acceptably and unacceptably in the phrase *maiden lady*. What I heard most often about Stella concerned her strangeness. *Odd-turned. Not right in the head.* The Stella stories were tinged with secrecy, and though I searched our family history, I was never able to find out very much about her.

At one point, I wrote a short story about Stella. The entirety of the story takes place on one day. Everyone has left the house, and she makes her way downstairs and out to the front porch, where she sits listening to the chilly fall wind coming down from the mountains. She sings a song I made up and put in her mouth: "The wind blows down, the wind blows back, the wind blows cold and that's a fact." In a later version of the story, I gave Stella a bell she hung from the porch rafters, so she could hear it even when she went back to her upstairs room.

The real Stella passed through the rips and tears in collective memory. I'm not sure if she was a Gray or a Calhoun, but I think she was my grandfather's aunt. I have no one to ask about her history, especially now that most of my ancestors are gone. This much must have been true: Glass back then wasn't exactly clear. Panes had waves and imperfections. Looking into an upstairs window from the yard, you must have seen only an impression, a ghost of a woman. Looking out through that beveled glass, Stella would have seen a subdued world, a hushed brilliance that passed as light.

* * *

As a writer of memoirs and personal essays, I've often confronted the question of what should or should not be told when it comes to writing truth. When I was writing a memoir about surrendering a child to adoption, more than one family member suggested that the story would be better written as a novel. I've many times heard criticism of my raw stories, ones that explore what happened when and why. During a recent trip back to Kentucky, a friend encouraged me to write a novel about my time in Greece many years ago. "Your kin must feel threatened," she said. "You've told so many of their secrets. Why not write fiction instead?"

I have written secrets, many of them belonging to my parents and cousins and ancestors. I've written about truths swept into corners, under rugs. The ends of marriages. Infidelity and reckless desire. I've explored pain, both my own and that inside the hearts of my kin. I've spoken my own history; I've given voice to other unspoken histories that have included mental illnesses. Schizophrenia, obsessive-compulsive disorder, bipolar disorder.

Are these stories a betrayal? Are they exploitation? I acknowledge that I've written hard truths, but my hope has been that the telling will provide answers. What does it mean, I've asked my pages again and again, to come from the center of a labyrinth and find one's way out?

Secrets fed me when I was small. Night scratching against the window screens. A light filtering beneath the door all night long. Those secrets had explanations I could oftentimes discover the next morning, but I was hungry for more. I write about certain events of my childhood over and over, as if the repetition is a spell that just might work if I figure out how. At twelve, I wanted to know what to call the fear I saw in my aunt's eyes—that time they held a cup of coffee to her lips, then walked her back and forth across the kitchen floor. I wanted to know why my grandfather came to live with us for six weeks when I was nine and what it meant when I overheard my mother whispering to my father: "Psych ward. Lithium. No choice." By the time I was thirty, one of my cousins had died after struggling with overwhelming depression. No one talked about how Greg died, but for months I dreamed of guns and ropes and deep water. Hunger grew inside me, an emptiness that pressed its little hands inside my chest. Even now, I want to know if it was real, the hunger I remember in the houses of my ancestors: an enormous, mangy bird with hard eyes that wanted and wanted.

* * *

Nancy Drew. Trixie Belden. A series of Judy Bolton books that involved a woman detective, a news reporter named Horace, and a cat named Blackberry. I loved reading about secrets. I soon graduated to more complex mysteries—Agatha Christie, Sir Arthur Conan Doyle, Dashiell Hammett. Those, too, soon grew unsatisfactory as I began to long for more intricate mysteries. "Look where we will," Wilkie Collins wrote. "The inevitable law of revelation is one of the laws of nature: the lasting preservation of a secret is a miracle which the world has never yet seen."

The mysteries became more intimate, more complex. After school, I waited long hours in the garage for my mother, who suffered from an unnamed mental illness, to let me come inside. I opened boxes of old letters and photographs I found on the shelves beside my father's hand tools. I read between the lines. "I love you, Pearlie," he wrote to my mother long ago. "I love you like no other woman." On Sunday afternoons, I went with my father to his office, where we both went to escape my mother, and I read books by the stack from a Department of Education Library on the floor above his. Libraries became my sustenance.

By twelve, I was reading with abandon and often with disregard for understanding what I read or why. Edith Wharton. Thomas Hardy. D. H. Lawrence. I read hungrily, devouring the intricacies of relationships, of grief and surrender. I wanted to learn how to solve the secrets right in front of me. I'd come upon my father sitting at his office desk, his head in his hands. What did the unfocused, angry light in my mother's green eyes mean when we came home a half hour late? Their voices on the other side of my own bedroom wall were a language I couldn't decipher.

* * *

Stella's days in her brother's house must have been similar, one to the next. Her room's spare light as she sponge-bathed the familiar lines of her own body. Perhaps she went to church on the occasional Sunday morning. Or perhaps that was too daunting an outing— voices rising in praise, hands clapping so fast sparks rose in the air. Maybe she had to work for days to come up with the courage to spend time alone in the kitchen, but surely, I imagine, she kept a delectable secret there—her love affair with the senses. The dough, sleek and oiled as she turned it out on a floured board. Her hands kneading, fashioning familiar shapes—a leg, a thigh, the soft and hidden skin beneath an arm. How her hands caressed and yearned.

In my imagination, desire drove her mad, and I don't mean the desire for a particular face, a pair of certain hands, or the taste of another person's mouth, though that might have been there too.

Let's say she once followed a woman with wavy black hair down a sidewalk in town. Trailed her inside a store that sold bolts of cloth, stood watching while the woman filled a paper bag with silver needles. How would it be, she wondered, to count the lines beside the woman's eyes with her fingers? To memorize her face with touch? Later, when she bought something—a paper tape measure she didn't need—the air where the woman had stood had the sweet scent of roses. Desire had so many names she turned over and over in her mouth. The untied lace of a boot. The sigh of a dress falling against the floorboards. The moon's muted light. She longed to gather up all the names she found for desire and swallow them whole. No matter how cold the night, she kicked her legs out from the covers and let her skin drink the air. There was no satiation. The room whispered secrets, and darkness gathered in the middle of her chest.

* * *

In the months before my cousin Greg killed himself, I'd been traveling in India. We made our way south from Nepal, through Uttar Pradesh, Bihar, Haryana, Rajasthan. On the surface of things at least, India was shockingly immediate. Evidence of the body was everywhere. Hands touched us, asking us to rent rooms, to change money, to buy hashish. Men defecated at the feet of temple gods. Inside a stall, women crouched, butchering a goat, the scent of blood rising in the stifling heat of summer. The dead were unconcealed, floating past us on the Ganges, lying spread-eagled in the river behind the Taj Mahal. Mourners painted their palms red and lit incense that choked the air with sweetness. When Paul and I got back to the United States, everything that had been so blatant in India resumed its secrecy. Muzak floated along the aisles of enormous grocery stores. Interstates were jammed with cars, their windows rolled up.

I'd been home a couple of weeks when I talked on the phone with my mother, who told me that my cousin had died and that a funeral had been held a few days before. What happened? I wanted to know. I remembered Greg the last time I'd seen him. I'd been visiting the trailer where he lived. His mother and mine and an aunt sat in the kitchen smoking Winstons, everyone ignoring the music booming from a record player in Greg's room. Sadness seemed to ooze out of him as he paced the kitchen, his black eyes damp and red, his curly hair raked back from his forehead. He stood by the counter, his boots tapping to an old Aerosmith song. He was the definition of wild, and I thought of the stories I'd heard about him—out of work at the mines, held up a train, on speed, fathered a baby.

Later, when I drove back to eastern Kentucky to visit, no one mentioned the word *suicide*. My mother and my aunt, Greg's mother, referred obliquely to something that had occurred, a something seemingly outside themselves. "When that happened to Greg," they said when the subject of death came up. What I gathered is that he'd shot himself in his bedroom. Another time when I visited my aunt's trailer, I used the bathroom in the bedroom that had been Greg's, and I studied the floor and the paneled walls, looking for unwashable bloodstains left by gunshot. Nothing was there. Death had happened, but it had been folded into a tiny secret and hidden inside a drawer no one would open again.

* * *

In a long-ago writing class at Upward Bound, a motivational summer program for high schoolers, students described secrets using only immediate sensory details. I spent my time getting to know as many of the students as I could—talking to them at lunch, asking to see their projects, checking on them if anything seemed amiss. From that writing class, I remember a description of a mouth hidden by a hand. A stretch of loamy soil, smoothed flat with a branch. Clouds obliterating the sun. The next part of the exercise was writing a page about releasing the secret. What did the mouth say when the hand was pulled away? Was the sunlight unadulterated happiness or something else? Our chairs pushed into a circle, we wrote quietly, and I occasionally looked up, studying them.

To one side of the circle was a girl I remember as big all over. She wore boxy, knee-length dresses and had large hands, long brown hair gathered in a big tangle on top of her head. The program was six weeks long, and during the weeks so far, the girl had sat by herself at lunch and underneath a tree during outdoor activities, arms circling her knees. During the group writing activity, she stared at the window, its long panes of dusty glass. Her lips moved, and she wrote a word or two, chewed at the end of a pencil. At lunch that day, I made a point of inviting myself to sit with her, asked to hear what she'd written about. I don't remember if she revealed her secret then or if it became obvious to all of us as the summer passed.

Her dresses began to seem less boxy. They stretched across a stomach that grew more ample, and what had seemed like voluminous silences began to make sense. She was pregnant, seven, eight months along, and the pregnancy was a secret she'd kept not just from us but from herself. She told the program coordinator that she had not known she was pregnant—that she didn't know how she'd conceived, not when or where. I still remember the piece she wrote in class: "A secret is a whole world inside me, keeping itself as quiet as it can."

* * *

In Charlotte Brontë's *Jane Eyre*, the secret in the attic of Rochester's mansion is a "savage" with black eyebrows, bloodshot eyes, reminiscent of "the foul German spectre—the Vampyre." The secret is a madwoman, mad, they say, because of a family lineage of mental illness, mad because of her dark, suspect race, mad because of her passionate (and unruly) Jamaican blood brought to live in the wild moors of England. Bertha Mason stands beside Jane's bed at night, laughing demonically, "a goblin-laugh," before she enters Rochester's room and sets fire to his bed curtains.

I read Brontë's novel many times as I was growing up, feeling the suppressed passion that Jane feels—the longing for recognition, love, touch—and the enormous power of the fire inside a woman's heart. I longed to look into Bertha Mason's face and make my own judgments about what savagery was, what madness looked like. I got that chance later, when I read Jean Rhys's *Wide Sargasso Sea*. That novel was rich with the overpowering scent of flowers from the island of Antoinette's childhood, the scent of sex and power. Antoinette becomes Bertha, mourns her own passion hidden away in a room, transformed into madness. Secrecy becomes rage, and rage becomes fire as Bertha looks at Jane's wedding dress on the floor, dreaming it into flames.

* * *

Two years after our world travels, Paul fell in love with a woman who grew perennials in the greenhouse where he worked. He nose-dived away from our relationship, never once talking about the whys and hows. I blamed myself for the demise of things. Heaviness filled my hands and feet with a sludge I resisted as I tried to carry on with my life, but some days I couldn't stop crying. I was drowning in depression even before Paul fell out of love with me, and after he left, I ended up for two weeks in a public rehab facility, the closest thing to emergency care my social worker/counselor could find for me on short notice. I played poker and watched Rambo movies in the break room with street people and heroin addicts. Then I checked myself out.

I took up the reins of my life again, furtively and with a discomfort like being inside another body. On a cold night, I cranked up a kerosene heater and went to make tea, returning to a room full of pale gray ash from the heater. Another night, as I talked at length on the phone, a soft thud resounded outside the kitchen window, and I looked up to see a huge black snake wrapped around the branch of a tree, swinging itself back and forth, back and forth against the window glass. The world was full of signs and dark wonders, but I couldn't read any of them. I lit candles every second day at an altar for the Sacred Heart at a Catholic Church in town. I prayed fervently, as if the world were a sealed box with the answers I needed, if only I could discover the key, but there was no key.

I had swallowed it, and it lay at the bottom of my heart, turning and turning, releasing sorrow into my blood. I kept Paul's photograph taped to the refrigerator, lined up a pair of his old shoes next to the door.

One afternoon in town, I ordered fast food. I sat in my pickup with my plate of chicken livers and coleslaw in an alleyway behind a bookstore, devouring the food as if my life depended on it, until someone I knew walked by and saw me. He waved at me, a sign of friendship, and started toward my truck. I stepped on the accelerator, frightened that the secret of my sorrow had been discovered and thus might vanish like so much else had.

* * *

A child's rhyme: "One is for sorrow, two for joy, three for a girl, four for a boy, five for silver, six for gold, seven for a secret, never to be told." As far as I know, Stella's life in an upstairs room remained a secret, except for rumors and offhand references I picked up and stored away over the years. Stella: the odd-turned, contrary woman. I will never know for sure why she spent her life locked away. Mental illness never diagnosed. An illness seen as a mysterious sign from

God or from the devil. And if not mental illness, something else. A choice about love or belief. Or something simpler but no less powerful. A woman full of so much power, so much radiance, it had to be contained somewhere. Perhaps Stella contained herself in that room, unwilling to share who she was and what she felt with a world she couldn't tolerate. I will never know.

What I do know is that I come from generations of secrets. An aunt suffered from seizures and visions. I remember her lying down in the afternoon—long naps with the covers pulled over her head in the heat of the day. Another cousin spent time in rehab, for what I'm not sure. She, too, became a suicide no one talked about. Silences were huge and deafening, and there were smaller ones, more hushed secrets. Curtains drawn. Doors locked. Contents of drawers and envelopes taken out when I'd visit, secrets discussed one by one. This man who left this woman. This hurt. That one. Suffering to snack on, to live with, day by day by day.

* * *

Secrets should never be told, but I have told them, have opened the drawers, read the letters, asked the questions. I've told the truth, at least my version of it. As a memoirist, I believe that reaching far inside, turning truths over and over in my own two hands, and translating them onto paper is as close as I can get to real faith. And by reaching far inside, I have come upon my understanding of the truths of others. Aunts. Mother. God, even. Some days, I think I know why Stella was locked away from the world. Other days, my words are only careful guesses that, I hope, honor what really happened, when.

My own truth is that I've spent over twenty years, off and on, seeking the professional services of counselors. I've opened my mouth and taken Communion, both the wafer of the Lord and the medications I have hoped will pull me back up from the dark waters of myself. I've prayed in grand cathedrals and in the parking lots of little churches I've passed on road trips. I've walked in graveyards and knelt beside markers where names and dates have long been illegible. I've hiked deserts and sat by the ocean, watching the waves go in, out. I've sought the consolation of everything from candles for the Blessed Mother that I light on my desk each morning to chants I listen to each night before I go to sleep. *Om Namah Shivaya.* I have bowed down to the truths as I came to know them.

Memoir is a difficult act. It is speaking. Speaking up. Speaking out loud. Memoir hurts, but it does not dishonor, nor does it disown. It may renounce the cruelties of one's past at the same time that it hopes beyond hope that there may be resolution, if not restitution. It speaks toward the truth, although it may never, ever uncover the deepest part of what is hidden. Maybe it's a song. The sound: *hush, hush, hush.* Each tone, every *h*, transforms as it leaves the mouth. *Hush* becomes *here. Here* becomes an invitation.

Memoir is not a ripping away of the comfort that secrecy can be. Secrecy is the security of those closed curtains midday. It is the darkness that holds us on a night that feels like it will never end. It is the unsaid, held inside our cupped hands.

We listen to what it has to tell us, and then, perhaps, we set it free.

* * *

I have vivid dreams, many of them about houses. Houses in Kentucky, North Carolina, Virginia. All the places I've lived and written about in order to come a little closer to uncovering the secrets of my life. I dream a small brown house and a creosote bridge across a creek. I dream the house on a lake where I lived alone for almost ten years, the path I walked down to a dock where I leaped into the warm Georgia waters. I dream kitchens, attics, a bedroom with a large stone fireplace. I dream the dull red shine of a tile floor. A beat-up screen door opens to a sunroom where I used to sit with my granny at breakfast. I don't think I've ever dreamed about Stella's house, though writing scenes in a memoir is a kind of dream.

In one such scene, there's tall summer grass, unmown until you reach the yard. The speckled orange lilies called flags are growing to one side of the house, and on the other side is a gate no one needs. A garden reaching farther than I know how to write. Instead I write myself walking up the front steps, across a small front porch. The chairs on the porch are inviting but tentative in a way I can't describe. Metal chairs, their green paint peeling, and thick spiderwebs in the porch eaves.

Then there's the small sound of a bell and a voice. "Stella," the voice calls. A screenless window is open, yellowed lace curtains blowing outside. After time passes, I write some more, carefully considering the weight of the secrets I am summoning. "Stella," I call again, and I wait.

VERTIGE

I remember that night like a painting of an off-kilter world. I was six, seven, and it was fall, our October trip home. Things in the house skittered and ticked, gnawed inside the walls, and I lay still between my sleeping parents, listening. When I opened my eyes, I saw a tangle of thin fingers scratching at the windows. Branches. Beside the window, on the wall next to my father, were streaks of brown on the wallpaper. By day, I'd run my fingers along the streaks. Watermarks, my mother said, but at night I remembered the stories of my uncle Roy's bleeding ulcer, and I could see him in this same bed, sick as a dog from drinking, as my aunts whispered. Two, three times a year, we rode three hours north, up from Harlan County, to visit my mother's people, a trip my father hated. "You love them more than me," he said when they fought hard. As I sat up, the brown streaks flexed and twined and straightened in the dark. The world was unclean with coal ash and human hands. My mother said it was so.

With the fiberglass window curtains drawn, I could barely see my father's face, his eyes small and squinty without their glasses. This was the bedroom where we always slept, one and two and three. On my other side, my mother woke, and she laid her hand along my leg, made a shushing sound to quiet me. She swung her legs over onto the floor, and I moved to the bed's edge, watching. We slid our feet into shoes and made our way through the open bedroom door out into the living room, where it was lighter with the pulled-back curtains. She held her fingers to her lips as we tiptoed through the dining room and past the doorless room where my grandparents and my uncle slept. We were quiet as we went through the kitchen and out the back door.

That night is soft with memory, tinged with the coal ash tipped by the bucket beside the path we followed down the hill. What I remember is the huge black sky and clouds and only a slipper of moon. "Walk beside me," she said. "Don't you touch a thing." My mother feared the unclean world—mud on the path, beggar's-lice from the weeds—so I clung to her down the path. Quick bat-shadows moved against the sky and the bare autumn branches as our feet found surety along the incline. At the end of the path, there were the rough boards and the door that swung open, the smack of scent against our faces, the smell of bodies and what they let go. I looked down into what she called nastiness, the heaps of what we had surrendered. "Mind me, now," she said as she lifted me up, sat me down atop the hole with its blackness and who knew what way down there. I was to be quick and to watch the tail of my nightgown, how it might trail in. While she sat on the other hole, I couldn't help myself. I reached out, touched the wall, felt shapes in the wood—mountains, a hole for a moon, a world like the one outside. We listened to the trickling down until we were done.

Back up the path and beside the kitchen door again, we stood beside the house. There it smelled like the garden earth my grand-mother turned with her hoe, and there was a clothesline. Towels and a shirt hung there catching the air, and beside the steps on an upturned crate, there sat a metal pan, in case the rain came. Rain-water, my mother always said, was the best thing; it made your face and your hair so soft. In my first class at school, I had even written a story about it, one my father put in a desk drawer because he was proud. "If you don't have a shower or a bathtub," it read, "then wash yourself with the rain." There was a shallow pool of rain in the pan, and it caught what light there was, and I remember how we stood looking as something invisible fell and made rings in the water. The world was black and enormous all around us, full of all my mother feared—soot and love and the unkind mouth of God. It was a world off-kilter, one I would not understand for years and years, and we watched it shiver in the rainwater's reflection.

* * *

The world spins and shivers in so many ways. Car lights pass closed blinds. The dog's closed eyes move, restless in sleep. A hand holds a cigarette and trembles on the way to a mouth. A woman wakes in midwinter with her heart racing, clicks the lamp on, and watches the room shiver with uncertain grief. I am forty-something, and I have driven fourteen hours east from Maryland to Kentucky, passing mountains and then pastures for racehorses, and I stop at a diner for coffee and grilled cheese. I am standing by my car, keys in hand, when I look across the road at pennants on a sign at a car sales lot waving in the hot summer wind. The pennants go taut and slack, taut and slack, and presto, the world begins to spin. Clouds pass the sun at a startling speed. The pavement beneath my feet shifts and circles, and I sink down beside my car door, holding on to my knees as I listen to my ears humming.

The medical condition where a person feels as if they or the objects around them are moving when they are not is called vertigo. Ver-de-go. "Be holp by backwards turning," Benvolio says in *Romeo and Juliet*. From early 1500s Latin, *vertere, vertigo* means, literally, *to turn*—whirling while one is stationary. It is a sickness involving motion. Giddiness. Dizziness. A sensation of unsteadiness and loss of balance, a feeling of looking down from a great height, and it can be induced by a change in head position: turning over in bed, lying down, looking up, stooping, or making any change in head position. It can mean blurred vision, nausea, hearing loss, and a lowered level of consciousness. In 1952, Margaret Dix and Charles Hallpike at Queens Square Hospital arrived at a symptomatological definition by their examination of some one hundred patients. "Giddiness comes on," they say, "when [the patient] lies down in bed or when [she] turns over in bed, or when such a position is taken up during the day; for instance, in lying down beneath a car or in throwing the head backward to paint a ceiling." The examiner grasps the patient firmly by the head and briskly pushes them back into the critical position, thus obtaining a reliable diagnostic story.

* * *

My most recent vertigo story began in 2016, the night of the Presidential. I started the evening with drinks and vote watching with friends on a farm where I stay a couple of nights each week while I'm teaching up in Gettysburg, Pennsylvania. My landlords are a couple who, like me, fully expected a big Hillary Rodham Clinton (HRC) win after the heat of the long political campaign. Unlike me, the landlords, Charles and Cornelia, were not necessarily HRC fans, and I had not revealed to them my musings about why it was that Donald Trump had the appeal he did—his fast-talking promises about making jobs and cleaning the house of politics for the working-class people like the ones I grew up with in eastern Kentucky. We all knew that Trump denigrated women, and I firmly believed that he was, as an Australian friend said, a flash rat with a gold tooth. We also knew that Trump had prepared two election-night speeches—a victory speech and a concession speech—but we were confident which victory speech we would hear: HRC's, delivered beneath a glass-ceilinged ballroom in New York City. By nine o'clock, all of us were onto our third glass of wine and watching the electoral votes anxiously, with HRC sliding lower and lower by the state, 209 to 244. Charles's mouth hung open with disbelief. "The bastards," he said. "The bastards."

By ten o'clock, I had slipped away to watch the rest of the election on my own. I crossed the big yard to the furnished cottage I rented and stood looking at the heavy clouds crossing the moon.

It had been an unseasonably warm winter so far, and the air was damp, near warm, tasting of rain. The grayness seemed to slide inside with me, where I poured one more glass of wine and then sat in bed with my laptop, live streaming the election results as long as I could stand them. I fell asleep that way, with the laptop's blue light, rain beginning and wind picking up across the pastures, keening as it circled the cottage.

When I woke, the blue screen had shut down, hibernating, but the room wasn't pitch black, though it was two or three o'clock. Upstairs lights were on at the landlord's house across the way, and the wind had died down. There was a steady rain, and I imagined threads of what might have been summer lightning in the fields, if it weren't November. I lay still, phrases from the night before echoing inside me. "If Trump wins," Charles had said, "maybe it won't be that bad." And in behind the snippets and bits of election-night returns speaking in my head, there was a phrase, one in a familiar voice, my grandmother's maybe, or that of a friend of hers whom she used to call Leora: *Witching hour. Witching hour.* I sat up, swung my feet out on the bedside rug, and flipped on the table lamp.

I can only describe the room as a dream made of tilting and whirling. The lamplight on the cottage wall trailed past, then picked up speed, gathering shadows and colors from the oil painting of red and blue flowers beside the chest of drawers. I tried to fix my attention on the dresser mirror, but the shine was too bright, and I shut my eyes, holding on to the edges of the bed. I could still think, and I thought of the magical carpet in the cartoon, the surprised faces of Aladdin and his pet monkey as they soared above the lights of the desert. I counted, one and two and three, up to ten, then opened my eyes to the web of light and dark on the walls, which were still moving, quicker now. The cottage's walls were lined with paintings, some from Cornelia's mother, and I concentrated on one of flowers, the layers of red and blue. My breath was fast and sweat grew at the base of my spine as I gripped the edges of the bed. My body was heavy enough to keep me steady, but nausea gathered inside me. I breathed, in, out, waiting for the night to become still.

* * *

Researcher and ophthalmologist Francis Heed Adler offers the first descriptions in medical literature of positionally induced vertigo, and his research, combined with that of Ernst H. Bárány, hypothesized that vertigo is a disorder of the otolith organs. Otoliths, also called statoconium or otoconium or statolith, are calcium carbonate structures in the inner ear, particularly in the vestibular labyrinth of vertebrates. In 1952, researchers Margaret Dix and Charles Hallpike extended the earlier work of Adler and Bárány via a study of some one hundred patients at London's Queen Square Hospital, arriving at a definitive test for positional vertigo. *Otoliths. Vestibulars. Labyrinths.* They say that by counting the growth rings on otoliths, one can estimate the age of rare types of fish. *Labyrinths. Vestibulars. Otoliths.* I say the words to myself like they are charms, spells, bones found in a cave. I can almost hear her, one of the patients Dix and Hallpike describe in their studies of vertigo.

She tells them how she was standing under the shower, the first time. The water roared, loud as the falls, and her heart picked up the sound, a deafening throb that followed her back to bed. She lay in the early morning light, listening. She exhaled, and her breath came out white, a shape of itself that grew larger, covered her, a heavy quilt. She spent the day like that, weighed down, waiting for the dizziness to subside, and it did, for the most part. For the next few days, she felt as if she were walking in someone else's body, an observer seeing from someone else's eyes. The earth was unsteady, at a drunken tilt, and she felt her way down the hall at a bookstore where she turned pages, looking for symptoms. "Positional nystagmus of the benign positional type." The words seem redundant. It is caused, the doctors tell her, by a disorder of the utricular macula. Neither the doctors nor the way they take hold of her, straighten her, turn and shift her head do anything to make her right. Their words tell her nothing about the way lines on the street flex and bend. The way the world sounds as if it were underwater. She wanted one word: *Still*.

* * *

Vertigo is by definition not just dizziness but also a disordered state of consciousness. I think of it as a sort of between world experienced in the middle of the night or at the edge of a sidewalk or right before I turn a corner. Vertigo is a simultaneous stepping back and stepping forward and a confusion about which direction is the stable one. I see myself at six or seven years old in the front seat of the car as we drove to Floyd County. My parents were on either side of me, their words crossing and recrossing me as they quarreled. Why, my mother wanted to know, had he taken her so far away from everything? "Everything" was my granny and pa's place in Floyd County, Kentucky, its smokehouse and well, its bottomland and its house of five rooms. My father was a schoolteacher, then a state administrator. He'd taken her and himself both out of the world they came from, set our family on the high road out, and yet my mother was always longing for where she came from, always looking back to roads leading home. It was a dizzying situation, to be neither here nor there.

For most of my life I, too, have been dislocated. I've moved some thirty-seven times. I've lived in eight states, fifteen cities, and dozens of houses and apartments and have driven an array of cars and trucks. When I last moved, I packed up eighty-some boxes of books, twenty-two boxes of memorabilia including postcards and napkins with the beginning of poems, crystals from old chandeliers, outdated fortunes from Chinese cookies. I have been a maid, a landscaper, a cook, a trail crew worker. I have been adjunct, lecturer, assistant professor, visiting professor, associate professor. I am on some fast track forward, and I hold on to the edges as my life moves and moves. I write stories that are poems, poems that are stories, novels that float and drift in time. I am a roadie, a pack rat, as disordered as they come. I am that child holding her mother's hand as we trudge the path back up from an outhouse in the dark. I am still standing beside her, watching the world's reflection trembling in a pan of rainwater.

* * *

In 1978, Gerry Conway, Trevor Von Eeden, and Vince Colletta introduced a new character into the DC Comics universe: *Count Vertigo*. Count Vertigo, the last descendant of a royal family ruling the small eastern European country of Vlatava, first appeared in Star City, where he tried to steal back the jewels his parents had sold when they escaped to England after the war. Victim of a hereditary inner ear defect that affected his balance, the count had an electronic device implanted in his right temple that corrected his balance. And then. Voilà! Vertigo learned that he could distort the perceptions of others. Donning a green and black costume inscribed with concentric circles, Vertigo had the power to alter lives. Up from down? Right from left? Right from wrong? Count Vertigo embarked on a life of balance-altering crime.

The count's ability to tinker with his inner ear device led him to duels with the Black Canary and Green Arrow, but his long-range disordering skills could, in fact, have been throwing lives off-kilter for years. Was it Count Vertigo hard at work with the dizzying promises of the last presidential election? On the one hand, promises to West Virginia and Pennsylvania coal miners. They'll start work again! Be proud once again to be miners! At the same time, Peabody, the nation's largest coal company, slid into Chapter 11 bankruptcy, following at least fifty others in the industry in the last few years, including Arch Coal, Patriot Coal, Alpha Natural Resources, and Walter Energy. In West Virginia—the heart of coal country—production has hit lows not seen since the strikes of the late 1970s, with the state losing more than 35 percent of its coal jobs since 2011.

But the power of Count Vertigo is far-reaching, if we look at the range of vertigo sufferers. Politicians. Sports figures. Writers. Visual artists. The likes of Emily Dickinson, Philip K. Dick, Peggy Lee, and Ryan Adams were or are all vertigo sufferers. No one, it seems, is safe.

* * *

Ginger has been used for centuries in Asia to combat seasickness. Legend has it that commercial fishermen at sea would chew on a slug of ginger root to ward off bouts of seasickness. "It's quite common today," says Dr. James Duke, an authority on medicinal plants at the US Department of Agriculture, "to see people in boats around Hong Kong munching on preserved ginger." Other lore suggests that dew can be gathered early in the morning and snuffed up the nostrils as a cure for vertigo, while other sources say that dew gathered from the leaves of fennel or celandine is an even more powerful remedy.

In my case, vertigo has been treated by the administration of powerful drugs. Bonine. Dramamine. Meclizine. Scopolamine. Promethazine. Metoclopramide. Diazepam. Lorazepam. The drugs are a litany of *n*'s and *m*'s, a veritable song of *a*'s and *o*'s and *zine*s. The drugs are available in the form of tablets that melt under the tongue like a soothing host. In the form of gel caps and neat triangular pills. They come in prescription bottles and in tidy vials easily slipped out of a bag for ingestion in the midst of a crowded party or tapped circumspectly underneath the disguise of a conference table. After a recent bout of vertigo, I was prescribed three meclizine tablets per day and as much sleep as possible. After two tablets, one in the early morning and one at noon, I sank into a kind of stupor in which I dreamed of other times and houses and highways and drove half-remembered roads, undizzied and inert.

But half-somersault canalith repositioning, also known as the Foster maneuver, has become the ritual with which I am most comfortable. When vertigo arrives unaware, as it most often does, the maneuver is a routine of being on one's knees, turning one's head at that position, then again, half-raised, then again, raised and head back, toward the ceiling. There are videos and instructions, but I have come to think of this maneuver as an act of kneeling and bowing, almost an act of supplication. Sometimes, with the room spinning, I kneel and shut my eyes and imagine the churches I went to so long ago. You'd come forward for the call to prayer, and sometimes you'd pray along with a dozen other people, all your voices rising, as you longed for them to lay their hands on your bowed head and bless you. To heal the off-kilter world, I remember it, remake it.

* * *

A medical report published in July 1990 contends that Vincent van Gogh was not mad, as has been speculated, but had a painful inner ear disorder that caused him to cut off his left ear and send it to a prostitute. Van Gogh himself writes to his brother of protracted, disabling attacks of what he calls *vertige*, accompanied by auditory hallucinations and aversion to light and movement. During these attacks, he writes, "I feel a coward before the pain and suffering." He also writes of long periods of calm, symptom-free, with no sign of the debilitating *vertige*.

I like to imagine van Gogh waking, pushing open the windows to extraordinary silver-white light. He must have breathed the light in, held it in his belly until it was an urgency he could not ignore, a desire already summoning a field of sunflowers. He was so full of light he left his room quickly, no time for his bowl of coffee, his tear from a loaf of bread. In my imaginings, I follow him down the streets of stones and corners, follow as he walked past the last house. Children played beneath the trees, and the sound of laughter drifted after him, stretching thin as he hurried past the red barn. A young woman sat there on a three-legged stool, her dress so blue he could taste it. The morning by then was drenched with that blue, and he was thankful for the web of clouds that softened the sky as he hurried, a lane full of houses, then two more fields, and he was there, at the edge of a yellow world.

Saffron. Ocher. Amber. He closes his eyes and recites every yellow name he knows, but no word is enough, and by then, the light is straight overhead and so strong he can think of nothing but his hands. He reaches and parts the sharp leaves. He plunges in. He strides. He heads for the center of everything, the center of yellow light. But of course there is no center. He walks and parts leaves, and his hands are burning with fine leaf cuts. By then his eyes and his ears and his heart are so full of light he is blinded. The world moves with sunlight, a color that fills his mouth, and he wants to sing it, but it is the world that hums and his ears full of sound. The heavy yellow blossoms themselves are only shapes, lines, circles, and threads of light that weave around him, lift him up, set him down again, spinning. He grabs hold as he falls into a world made of the motion of sunflowers. Days pass, and he writes to his brother, "Life passes like this, time does not return, but I am dead set on my work."

* * *

The world shivers and spins. "Climate change denied," the NPR commentator says. "Immigration denied from six Muslim-majority countries. Major health care policy denial in the works. Subtle denials for LGBTQ workers. Miners who voted this administration in will not find a brave new world of coal." For weeks after the presidential election, I wake regularly at 3:00 a.m., scrolling in the dark past the news of such disorder. I prefer the reading of news on my phone these days, the quick movement past enmity after enmity, but one morning as I scroll, I can feel the edges of it. The phone casts shadows on the wall past my bed, and they quiver, a sign. My heart picks up, fluttering, skipping beats, and I breathe, in, out, calming myself. I have grown used to the way vertigo sneaks in, how alert my body has become to the disruptions of its rhythms. My ears are alert for sounds, the call of any night birds, the bend and scratch of branches against the cottage walls, the hum from inside my brain.

I have learned to recognize the signs of vertigo's approach, and if I am still enough, if I breathe, wait, sometimes it drifts on past, a visitor waving farewell. I lay the phone down beside me, turn on my side, try to focus, but the world feels huge. The four corners of the room in the farmhouse cottage are round with shadows, and from the window in the room beyond this one, the edges of light from the field flicker. I focus, remembering the headlines I've read on my phone, one headline amid the chatter, a piece I read. "The sky has changed." Inuit elders say that the earth has shifted, wobbled. The elders declare that the positions of the sun, moon, and stars have all changed, causing changes in the temperature. The sun is higher, warmer. The wind is stronger, the weather harder to predict. The world, they say, has now tilted.

If I act quickly, I tell myself, I can keep the vertigo at bay. In my bedside drawer is a vial of the meclizine. Beside my bed is a clear floor space where I can kneel, maneuver my head to the right and to the right again, until undizziness comes. Or maybe I can get up in time. I can feel my way across the room to the painting I admire most. I love to stand in front of it and study the red petals of the flowers, the solid, slender vase. I could get up now, if I'm quick, and feel my way to that painting in the dark, lay my hands against the thick edges of the paint, the lines and swirls, the shadows and spaces and light and dark. Between the red, painted world in the dark and the huge, tilting world beyond, there just might be a still space, one that I can slide into and hold on to for a little while.

* * *

Of course, what happens on nights like this, on nights when vertigo happens, is that I am spun backward in time, taken back and back. That one night. Was there a half-moon? Did it shine between the branches of the stone pear tree in the bottomland by the outhouse? Did light shimmer and break in the tin pan of rainwater for washing my mother's hair? The night was a broken mirror in the dark, a world made of fragments that I reorder into beauty in my memory. But it was not. That world was a rusted-out wringer washer beside a five-room house, the bodies of butchered hogs hanging up in the smokehouse. My grandmother's palms, red from sulfur water, hands red from the shirts she scrubbed, her back bent over a washboard. That world was hard, lean, poor. By day my grandfather was a deep miner, and so was my uncle, and my cousins and their cousins, and so on unto now, a broken world made of who owns what and who does not. And at forty, fifty, I am still climbing that path back up in the dark. "Don't touch anything," my mother says, and I am still trying to obey. Climb the hill up from all of it, and don't look back. And yet I do, again and again and again. I am dizzy with the looking back and ahead, back and ahead to who I was and who I am not and who I am.

THE LAND BETWEEN

1.

A storm is in the distance, and we're between worlds. Dusk and sky. Heat and cool as we swim across the cove. My students are at my house for writing and dinner, and now I'm swimming to the far shore of the lake with the one who writes about the jungles of Peru, about ayahuasca ceremonies, rituals for cleansing the soul. As I swim I think about the soul, about the waters where I grew up. Water was for soaking beans. It was for cooling off in the river, like in a picture I have of my grandmother and grandfather, fully dressed and sitting in a shallow spot, arms around each other. Water in the mountains was for baptisms and redemption. I float on my back, letting the waters hold me.

I breaststroke, freestyle, backstroke as prestorm lightning streaks the sky. Birds hover and dive. Student voices drift across the lake. Back on the dock, there are five or six of my students, sipping wine and talking poetry and prose and the places they'll all go next, after this last master of fine arts year. *Risk. Bring the story to fruition.* Another burst of lightning, and I scissor kick, tread, and rest, thinking about which comes first, lightning or thunder. The sky contracts, and the atmosphere shifts. Leave the pool as soon as the thunder comes, they always say. Don't stand near trees. Electrical discharge seeks out the shortest path.

The Georgia night floats over my skin, and I think of John, my husband, who lives fourteen hours from me. I remember how once, on this very dock, during another storm, I said, "Do you think there will ever come a time when we can make storms arrive when we want them to?" He is Monacan, a tribe from Virginia. He believes in the power of the Creator. "Controlling storms? You'd better hope not," he said. On the dock, someone whistles, sharp and loud, and I reposition myself, swim toward the voices.

2.

Beneath Liberty Lake, north of Baltimore, are copper mines, quarries, old roads, and a town once known as Mineral Hill, today mostly a patch of blacktop along Bollinger Mill Road. In Alabama, the town once known as Irma is beneath the waters of Lake Martin. Irma once had a post office designed by Frank Lloyd Wright. In Arkansas, there's a water-filled gorge known as the Narrows, with a town called Higden underneath it. In the 1800s the land was purchased by the government and the city abandoned, but eyewitnesses still report houses and streets, an underwater ghost town. In Oklahoma, there's Woodville, reported to have 360 residents in 1944, when it sank into yet another underwater ghost town. In Georgia, where I live, there's Lake Lanier. That lake, built in the 1950s, has beneath it an old dirt racing track. Foundations of buildings. Sunken cars and boats. Even a stretch of Georgia Highway 53.

3.

Nights by the lake when I can't sleep, I punch my Dream Machine alarm clock and play ocean sounds. I dream of shores I've seen. Greece. The cold clay beaches of England. The hot sands beside northern Australian reefs. Waves and fins. Salt water and fresh. And most of all, waves and waves of words.

In Georgia alone, seven years of teaching. Fourteen terms. Thirty-five workshops. Ten times four times five times seven workshop pieces read. A dozen fine arts projects, 150 pages each. Two literary magazines. Websites. Submissions. Contests. Conferences and residencies. Readings and lectures. Applicant files. Enrollment predictions. Faculty meetings. School meetings. Department meetings. End of year reports. Tenure files. Promotion files. Eight months of chemo treatments, five days a week of radiation treatments, three years of climbing out of illness. Some days, I think I am drowning.

On some nights when I can't sleep, I get up and sit at my dining room table. I turn on my laptop to blue screen light, its own body of water, unnatural blueness through which no living soul could swim. I stare into the screen and try to see some unfamiliar ocean's bottom, some silty lake floor. I try to tell myself that writing is an act of prayer.

4.

Having moved through cancer treatments, I've been tired a lot, unfocused and uninspired. I've needed something solid to set down in the middle of the workshop table. I've brought in a carved wooden iguana from Australia, and my students hand it from one to the next as a kind of talking stick that ostensibly means that no one can interrupt. Tonight the stick passes from hand to hand, until one young man is ready to be heard. Someone slides the iguana across the table, and he picks it up. "I just don't think this is a story yet," he says. "What's at stake with this story? Are you risking enough?"

I find that I'm having a hard time listening to the conversation, which is about craft. We're talking about interruptions in the voice of the story. About front-loading the plot. About dialogue. Place. Character. What I'm really listening to is far down somewhere inside me, and I'm trying to remember exactly what it is. A chair blew off the dock yesterday at the lake, and I watched it drift out over the water, then submerge, disappear. Or blue herons. How they hold themselves out, a straight line of gray and wings, then dip down, suddenly disappearing in their act of foraging. So many things disappear that way in the waters of the lake. The flip and dive of fish. Turtles and snakes. The circles and waves human beings leave in the wake of their speedboats and Jet Skis.

What I wish I knew how to do is bring magic to the stories we're discussing. *Magic* is a dubious word for the workshop table, but it exists inside me. There's me, standing in the warm house, out back at my grandmother's. In there were canned tomatoes and beans and a deep bin full of potatoes for the hard winter months. The building was kept cool by a spring that fed under the floor. I'd stand at the edge of the hole and look down and imagine forever. There's my father, skipping stones across a lake, with ring joining ring across the water. There's my aunt Ruth's shoulders, wet with the waters of faith as she was lifted up on the day she was saved. There's me standing now on the dock beside my house, casting my voice over the waters, hoping against hope that it comes to me, a story fully formed. How to bring *that* to the table in a writing workshop? The story and the heart converging, whole?

5.

In Georgia, there are eighteen lakes, the majority of them human-made. Manufactured lakes are impoundments—water accumulated in reservoirs—that do not occur naturally in the landscape. To create Georgia's human-made bodies of water, there have been displacements. Bridges. Plantations. Houses. Graveyards. For the construction of Lake Lanier, for example, seven hundred families were relocated. Channels were blasted. Powerhouses constructed. A river was diverted through the open gates. Saddlebacks set in place until the gates were closed and the lake began the slow process of filling.

6.

When I was swimming at the public pool years back, a sculptor named Esther swam up to me one day, holding her hands up to my face like a frame, and asked me to model for her. These years later, when I swim, I make a frame for this lake world. Million-dollar Georgia homes in the distance. Two roads in the distance, smaller houses and trailers beside them. Beside my own house, woods with a lone grave marked 1897. The sole piece of land owned by a former slave. Her family refuses to sell to make way for another lake house lot.

I tread water, and what I frame between my hands is smaller. The red door on the cabin near the long dock straight across the cove. The pattern in a cloud in the clear sky. A crane feather that drifted down from the air, now nothing but a spine. A child's swimming mask, blown off a pontoon and floating out. If I could, what I'd frame is one word. *Sunlight. Shadow. Ripple.*

I ask for this in my writing. "What," I say, "is this piece about? What is its heart?" I call that thing we try to describe transcendence. What makes the words rise off the page? Transcendence, I tell them, lies in the heart. In the belly. It is as elemental as earth, as fire, as air, as water. Can one word represent it at all?

7.

Many times when I swim in the cove, I think about a film I love. *Night of the Hunter,* based on a script by James Agee. Shelley Winters meets Robert Mitchum, the tattooed-hand preacher who tries to steal her fortune and finally leaves her under the waters of a lake, "down there in the deep place, with her hair waving soft and lazy like meadow grass." She could be at this lake's bottom, with other lost things. That chair I used to own. Flat stones I've thrown, making rings on the lake's surface before sinking to depths I've never seen.

All the words I've shed. A thousand conversations about words. The threads of a hundred lives not my own, and a thousand pages turned by other fingers.

As I swim, words grow still. They dive. Vanish. Become stories. In one such story, I am a woman not myself. She lives, that woman, in a house beneath the lake. She sits in that impenetrable world, that woman, on a front porch, in a glider, her hair flooding back in the same watery light that warms me as I swim. On her knee, a cup. Steam rises from the cup, trails through the depths of lake water and algae and the nipping mouths of fish. The steam becomes a rope of light she could grab to travel up from the lake's impenetrable bottom.

8.

All stories are water, really. Begin with one word on a page.

Lake.

The word *lake* comes from Middle English *lake* ("lake, pond, waterway"), from Old English *lacu* ("pond, pool, stream"), from Proto-Germanic **lakō* ("pond, ditch, slow moving stream"), from the Proto-Indo-European root **leg'-* ("to leak, drain"). Cognates include Dutch *laak* ("lake, pond, ditch"), Middle Low German *lāke* ("water pooled in a riverbed, puddle"), German *Lache* ("pool, puddle"), and Icelandic *lækur* ("slow flowing stream"). Also related are the English words *leak* and *leach*.

After the first word, ride the waves, sentence to sentence. Do they rise and fall? Think of the luscious lines, paragraphs, and pages of Ralph Waldo Emerson. "Wherever snow falls, or water flows, or birds fly, wherever day and night meet in twilight, wherever the blue heaven is hung by clouds, or sown with stars, wherever are forms with transparent boundaries, wherever are outlets into celestial space, wherever is danger, and awe, and love, there is Beauty, plenteous as rain, shed for thee, and though thou shouldest walk the world over, thou shalt not be able to find a condition inopportune or ignoble." Birds meet twilight. Blue heavens, scripted with stars. Each sentence meeting the next sentence, beauty and rain synonymous. I ride those sentences like waves. Transparent, he says. Another water lesson. *Beauty*. Celestial space become earth. Awe become here and now.

If Emerson is too transcendent, try the shallows at the shoreline of a particular lake. Find the nitty-gritty. Mud, dank and brown with summer's end. The yellow-green lines of September's pollen, washed up, a divide between water and bank. Wade in and watch what could float past. The effluvium of the fishing world. A left-behind Styrofoam bait bucket next to the dock, with earthworms and silvery tabs from beer cans. A bobber or two and the odd tangle of fishing line. A hook buried in the clay right next to your toes. A fish head. The razor-sharp edges of mussel shells.

If this lake world is still not specific enough, take it apart a little more. Limnology is the study of inland waters. Limnology tells us that lakes can be divided into three zones: the sloped area close to land; the open-water zone, where sunlight is abundant; and the deep-water zone, where little sunlight can reach. The depth to which light can reach depends on the density and size of suspended particles in the water—sedimentary or biological—and these color the lake waters. Decaying plant matter lends yellow or brown, while algae cause greenish water. Iron oxides make water reddish brown. In the waters, algae and detritus. Bottom-dwelling fish stir the mud in search of food. Other fish devour the plant eaters. And all of this in the light, dark world of surfaces and depths and all the watery world in between.

Stories have people and voices. For this particular story, pick a particular morning, a particular slant of light. Out the windows of the house, see the boat just beyond the dock. A girl and her father, fishing in the just-before-dawn. Step out onto the deck of the house and listen. The girl is laughing. They're playing music. Patsy Cline. "I Fall to Pieces." Watch the girl bend over the side of the boat, trail her fingers through the water. Even from far away, on the deck and with the early morning fog, the girl is so beautiful. See how she looks down into the still waters, wondering how far they reach, whether there is such a place, the faraway bottom of a lake.

9.

In 1990, a construction crew building a support for a bridge across Lake Lanier found a submerged 1952 Ford sedan. Inside were the skeletal remains of two women, Delia Mae Parker Young and Susie Roberts, both missing since April 1958. Workers clearing debris from the lake bottom found the car, its tires still inflated with air, the chrome hubcaps shiny, and the ignition and radio switched to on. A story unfolded. How that night in 1958 Susie and a companion drove to a local roadhouse, the Three Gables, where they enjoyed a few drinks. How they filled Susie's car up at a gas station and left without paying. How a watch found in the Ford sedan, all those years later, was set at 11:30.

10.

In the film *The Piano*, a nonspeaking woman named Ada travels in the 1850s to New Zealand for an arranged marriage. The husband is a distant man who has no understanding of the music Ada feels in the palms of her hands. Ada takes a lover who knows how to listen. When the husband discovers her unfaithfulness, he cuts off her index finger, trying to take away her music for good. Finally, late in the film, as Ada leaves the island, she insists that Baines, the lover, throw her piano overboard into the sea. As the piano sinks, she puts her foot into the loops of rope trailing into the water, and she is pulled deep under the waves, connected by the rope to the piano. At the last minute, she kicks free, rising through water into light.

11.

A storm happens when light air rises quickly into higher, colder air, creating drafts that sometimes reach over a hundred miles per hour. And then there's lightning. Air carries charged water droplets upward to heights where some freeze into ice and snow particles. Clouds form. As these particles begin to fall back to earth, charges within the cloud become mixed. The differences in charge are released as lightning. A single lightning strike over a body of water can deliver a billion electron volts and a hundred thousand amps. Strikes touch water, spread out, and penetrate the depths, touching everything alive.

Storms are what I will remember most of all from my time by that Georgia lake. The day the storm swept, white and heavy, across the waters, I could see it coming as I stood by the windows inside my house. Strong wind picked up the rowboat I owned, flung it across the yard. Wind that pushed so hard at the unlocked door in my living room I had to stand against it with my whole body. Rain drummed on the roof, wanting its way inside. Another day, down on the dock as I watched the storm's wide hand move forward. How the wind stilled, that day. Such silence and the slate-gray waters. A long vein of lightning flashed, and the sky became the belly of the earth. The world was so still I forgot to breathe.

12.

I've begun to inhabit not just a land between water and shore, between workplace and house, but between soul and self. *Soul.* That word, I'm told, is to be used sparingly in our age of the bottom line. There by the lake, I've dreamed soul. A preacher's hands reaching out, waters flooding from the long, wet sleeves of his robe. How I held my breath as he lowered me. *In the name of Jesus. In the name of the Father.* My legs kicked, and I reached up toward the light. *This is light of God forever and ever, amen.*

I have been soul-sick. With cancer's subsiding hiss inside me, and inside me a torrent of words. Stories and essays and poems and meetings and readings and my own voice inside one more room. Classroom. Hotel room. Boardroom. Bedroom with the shades drawn at the end of a long day and the distant sound of thunder over a lake. "You must show up whole," a friend wrote to me. "Show up whole for readings. Show up whole for friendship. Show up whole for writing. Show up whole for cooking and walking and filling the bird feeder." My soul's room has been empty, and I lie at night listening to a faraway amniotic sea.

13.

I have traveled the world searching for water and light. In the South of France on Bastille Day, I watched Roman candles exploding over the sea. In the North of India, I watched lit pyres float out over the Ganges, bodies on their way to ash and bones. Back home again, I watched my grandmother's hands light newsprint and coal in the grate in the back room of the house I thought of as home. And the memory of water. Water poured into a basin over the feet of believers in church. *And shall we believe in this, the fire of the Holy Spirit?* Amen.

All these years later, I try to teach via fire, via water. Like my grandmother and her mother and the ones before that, I try to lay on hands. What, I ask my students, is the heartwood? *Heart.* They imagine lace and arrows and cutouts in pink and white. Lay your hands against the pages, I tell them. Reach in. Pull meaning up from the depths. If you are afraid, be afraid. Ride the waves of intention. Let the inner life and the act of story converge.

14.

My very last afternoon at the lake house, I sit out on the dock with my sweetheart and with two students who've come to help me pack. We sip cold beers and dive into the chilly late spring waters. I swim far out, my lungs shocked by the almost cold, the patches of warm. Beside me, waves and sound, a boat and water affecting distance. I hold my breath, push my body down as hard as I can. I pass shadows of tree limbs, strands of grass. Threads of moss. My arms push through pale green sunlight.

I swim through all the seasons. Spring and clear cold. A trail of goslings. The lanky crane with its wild white mane. Summer and the boats returning. How they wave to me, the lone woman on the dock. The summer lake, full of fireworks and random country songs from passing motorboats. Cold bottles of water down from the house. I lie on a float out in the water and dream. Dream my way to the listless dog days of August. A cakey layer of pollen on the surface of the deep. Water turtles on hot, dry patches of earth beside the cove. Autumn and the air smelling of creosote and burning leaves. And that time, the cold season, I am the woman living alone beside a cove in winter. The slope of grass beside the lake. Arms full of kindling back to the hearth. Guests come for red potato soup and wine. She keeps herself warm in a bed laden with quilts her grandmother stitched by hand.

If I could have pushed past that last day, reached it, the heart of water, what might I have seen? Some vast city, maybe, five thousand years old. Pottery shards and walls, beads and sculpture, human bones, teeth. Is the farthest reach of water a void? Or is there a brilliance underneath the world so amazing we just might reach it if we understood how? I held still then, at the lowest point I could reach, looking up at the faraway surface. Thoreau says this about the surface of water: "I have discerned [there] a matchless and indescribable light blue, such as watered or changeable silks and sword blades suggest, more cerulean than the sky itself."

15.

The last days in the lake house, my back ached and my arms were bruised from the boxes I carried to a truck out by the road. Boxes of papers and pots and pans, shoes and towels, dishes and knickknacks, all the paraphernalia of years of a life of indecision. What were the choices in those boxes? Stay at a job that left me empty? Risk a life where I wrote but a life of the very poverty I'd come from in the first place, before I climbed the ladder toward success? Nights at the lake house, I filled seventy-five boxes with the books I was keeping, the notebooks I could not bear to throw away.

When I remember that lake time, I remember questions about the heart, both my own heart and the hearts of the pages I encouraged as they were born. I remember the question I keep, even now: *Can the writing of stories be taught?* Find the heart of your piece, I said. And I meant the deepest place. Find the heart and follow it, I said. That last lake day, I dog-paddled up to the ladder to the dock, felt the thick barnacles on the ladder's rungs. I'd lived beside the lake enough seasons to know the plankton and sediments by touch, the way they'd eaten away with rust what had once been new metal.

I wish I could tell you that my departure from that time and place was an act of magic. That I vanished, whoosh, and reappeared some other place, new and irrevocably whole. Now that I have moved away from that lake to the suburbs outside of a series of cities in the North, I write stories about that lake time, pages gathered from the waters. How, I ask, do women imagine transcendence? The eyelids of children fluttering as they suckle and sleep. Or that day I pulled myself up onto the dock and lay staring at water and sky.

HOW SOULS TRAVEL

March 12, 2020. I'm in Concourse B for an early flight out of Baltimore, and I'm watching news reports. Norwegian prime minister Erna Solberg announces a national lockdown. Dow Jones falls by 10 percent. The number of US cases of the new coronavirus is 984. That's 774 more cases than the night a week ago when my father died of a massive heart attack. That night John opened the door, and light spilled across our bed. "Your dad has passed," he said. Now I'm huddled next to the tall windows overlooking the airfield, hoping the plane to Kentucky is on time. I'm grateful for the protective mask I'm wearing, in case I'm crying. I tried to cry after my father died, with John as he lay next to me, stroking my hair. "I know," he said as I sat staring at the television screen.

Soon those with special needs are boarding. I am in zone four, one of only twelve passengers, so I think about taking two seats to stretch out in. A tall man is across the aisle from me, and he is up, down, up, down, wiping the arms of his seat and the let-down tray. He coughs, and I move to another seat in the almost-empty plane and sit staring at the blue rubber gloves covering my palms.

Two days ago, when John woke me, I was dreaming. In the dream my father said, "It was born in the caves of Asia."

* * *

1989. Paul and I were in a cheap and good Nepalese guesthouse arguing about how much cash we had left. My stomach was rumbling, a precursor to the giardia I didn't know I had, and I'd slept only a few hours in the muggy heat. I took my pinkish tea out onto the balcony, stood watching the world wake up. Bells jangled on the cart an old man pushed past. A bicycle veered into an alleyway. Across the square, a young woman stood on an overturned bucket, her feet bare, her black hair streaming down her back. She was wailing, a high-pitched and unadorned grief. I remembered my dream from the night before, the dream I often had. The creosote covered the bridge. My grandmother's house, thousands of miles away back in eastern Kentucky.

* * *

My plane lands, and I make my way to the gate for the connecting flight to Louisville; the terminals are not quite as empty in Atlanta as they were in Baltimore. People give one another wide berths, and I think of the phrase from last night's news: *social distancing*.

A woman hurries by, tugging her suitcase along, looking not so much socially distanced as furtive. My mask fogs my glasses, and I adjust it, keep walking along a conveyor belt to the next terminal. This person's eyes are averted; that person walks straight toward me, then veers away. Is this how a pandemic feels? *Pandemic*. I've looked pandemics up on several sites. Flu, 1918. Third cholera pandemic. *Pandemic*. A thing that is everywhere. A word that is hot in my mouth.

On the next plane, the air from the vent feels suspicious, and I close my eyes to pass the time to Louisville, where my stepmother will pick me up. Jean has been in my life since I was fifteen. She has been a devoted partner to my father, but in these last two years, my father told me, Jean has changed. She went to get the mail first every morning and came back in, envelopes hidden in her pockets. She spent hours talking on the phone in the room she had moved into in the basement. She closed doors. Bought new clothes. Came home at odd hours, all of it for that sales rep at the Pontiac dealer. He was sure of it. "Maybe I'll buy me a trailer," my father said. He'd move up the head of some holler back home, be to himself. Leaving her was a lie he told himself. "I can't imagine not loving her," he said to me in the months before he died.

I tuck his hurt inside myself as we land, and I make my way to ground transportation. I see Jean standing beside her red car. "I'm so glad to see you," she says, her chin trembling as she begins to cry.

* * *

My first experience with grief was a funeral. I was little enough that my feet dangled from the pew as I sat up straight to see my great aunt Het running up and back down the length of the church aisle. It was summer, and the windows were open to the scent of pink blossoms from the trees. Het ran with her hands raised, praising. "Pappy, Pappy," she shouted as she reached the end of the aisle and threw herself across Joe's body, with his black suit and the caves of his cheeks. "Lord, take me instead of him."

Most of my other early experiences with grief are also sounds. My cousin Jenny's sobbing as friends led her up the aisle at the funeral home on the day of my aunt Ruby's burial. Some voices are quieter.

My mother's crying on a Thanksgiving when my father stayed at the office all day. The way we sat that night, my father and mother and me, the television playing sitcoms, the silence underneath. How he reached his hand out to me. "Just a touch," he said, as if I would know what to do to assuage his marriage's sadness.

* * *

Before I arrived, Jean and I made a plan for a celebration of life. Photographs of our pasts with my father. A consultation with the pastor at their Baptist Church. A slideshow. Hymns to be sung and friends to tell stories about knowing him. Back at my home in

Maryland, I looked through boxes to find the right photos to send. A boy swimming in a river beside his brother. A young man riding a bicycle through the streets of a city in North Africa, his air force days. Today I have brought a poem to read at the service, a blessing by John O'Donohue: "May a slow / wind work these words / of love around you, / an invisible cloak / to mind your life."

Tonight we go back and forth over what is safe for the celebration, given COVID-19. Foods scooped from the same bowls will mean contact, and we no longer know what contact is contagious and what is not. We watch golf, one of Jean's favorite shows, and I feel lulled by the tiny balls sailing distances. I am exhausted as I make my way upstairs to the guest room. I toss and turn.

When I finally sleep, I dream I am one of several children coloring eggs we take out of a large metal bucket. Jean comes into the kitchen and looks disapproving. "You'll know when there's enough grief," she says. We decorate one last egg, cover it in construction paper to make it look like a blue bird. Jean gently touches the paper bird, the egg inside spoiled.

"My father is dead," I say aloud as I wake, wishing these words were something I could see or touch. I lie in bed, reading the daily news on my phone. The number of reported cases of the virus has gone up to 1,264.

* * *

That first Kentucky morning, I stand for a long while in the doorway of the room that had become his. The neatly made bed. The desk with its envelopes and ink pens and black-and-white composition notebooks. I open his desk drawer and find a small tin of rubber bands, an envelope full of news clippings. On a shelf near the bed are books with paper-clipped pages, bookmarks, and, in a copy of Thoreau's *Walden*, his neat handwriting. "God's glory is great," he has written. Next to the shelf is a mat with his shoes. The shoes are unlaced, their toes scuffed. I can hear him walking up the steps to this room, step-stop, step-stop, his feet hurting him. The abandoned shoes have mouths, and I seem to hear a sound come from inside them, as if my father is mourning his own absence.

* * *

In French, the word is *douleur*, and in its Proto-Indo-European origins, it is derived from the root *delh*, which means *to divide*. French mourning customs include the six days to make the decision of whether the deceased should have a cremation or a burial. In Ancient Greek, the word is *penthos*, meaning *uncountable*. Those mourning customs mean that Orthodox widows may wear black for up to two years, while a memorial service is held on the Sunday closest to the fortieth day after the death. Thailand's word is *khwām şeñā şok*, and the colors of grief there are purple for a widow and black for the mourners. Nepali uses the word *soka*, and its definitions include *the flame of fire* or *burning grief, the fire of sorrow*. No single language gives me the word for the grief hovering over the world these weeks. My father's death is a hole in the center of my chest, but I feel no particular sorrow, no specific pain I can name. The world itself is grieving. Today the number of those lost to the virus is 1,678, and when I read that number, my mouth goes dry. Can loss be counted? Do souls take flight?

* * *

I don't know which part of my father to mourn. His body is now nothing but ashes, but I remember his hands, the same nervous habit I have of nail biting. His round belly, a blanket draped across his lap. His feet, small, like mine. In his desk, I find a stack of his short stories. "By Clarence Salyer and kept for his daughter." His favorite is tagged with a Post-it: "Suwon, Korea—October 27, 1952."

Like the others, it is wistful, full of a longing for other times. There's a photo. The two of us standing at a kitchen counter, me in a striped sweater and him in a suit coat and tie. In that photo, it has been fifteen years since the surrender of my son to adoption, and I am on the verge of traveling the world. My father doesn't want me to go; he fears the foreign worlds I'll see, distrusts the man I'll be traveling with. "Would it mean anything if I told you not to go?" he asks, and I say no, say it would mean nothing at all. In the photo there is so much distance, so much that has happened and will happen, it will take us years and years to begin to talk about it.

* * *

Six feet is the recommended distance between people, but in Kroger Jean and I weave in and out of laden grocery carts, dodge people hurrying to stock up on hand sanitizer and toilet paper. The shelves for both are nearly empty. We stop at a restaurant for a quick lunch with her friend Sherry, where we exchange ideas about how to make our own disinfectants and discuss how Jean might move out of that big old house. "Nothing for at least a year," Sherry says as she pats Jean's arm.

After lunch, we drive to the funeral home to pick up my father's ashes, a cardboard box that rides in my lap as we drive across town. Graefenburg is where their church is and where the celebration of life will be. No one is there, but the church door is unlocked, and Jean and I go in, check out the sanctuary. We have no idea how many will come to honor my father, but we imagine the pews filled with mourners. "Will a distance between families keep everyone safe?" I ask as we head out to the car. Behind the church, a field is filled with waving grasses. The wind is chilly as I stand there holding the box of ashes, which I find comfortingly heavy.

* * *

I did not become the Baptist I was raised to be. I was not Roman Catholic or Episcopalian or Quaker or any of the other faiths I'd sampled over the years. But in all the churches in all those countries, I'd lit candles in cathedrals, temples, and roadside shrines for my baby boy, who existed nowhere I could imagine. I collected relics from every country. A stone. A feather. A shell in which I could see the face of God. I was a far journey from the God my father exalted, like the one in a story of his titled "Baptist Men's Day." "A Baptist man will lead," my father wrote, "both in his church and in his home, for our children and our future as a nation as God-committed Christian men."

The closest I ever came to describing God was images of the Holy Mother. I loved her face, both serene and devastated with the knowledge she'd always had of her son's death. In one Nepali city where we stayed for a week, I was surprised to find a small shrine to Mary. There I lit a candle and knelt in the packed dirt of the road. Head in my hands, I prayed, as I always did: "Holy Mary, Mother of God, pray for us sinners, now and at the hour of our death." In my deepest self, I was a fabric of holy things, things I'd tried and discarded. No song of the spirit had truly entered my heart.

That day at the shrine, there was a group of Buddhist nuns. They, too, lit candles, and then their voices rose into one voice and traveled out into the crowded streets of Kathmandu. I reached for the sound as if I could catch it and hold on.

* * *

On my second day in Kentucky, I tell Jean that I will read two poems at the celebration of life. The first was written by my father about his wish to have his ashes scattered at Dewey Lake. "I would favor some early morning / with only a slight breeze / but if this is not agreeable / decide according to the mood / of your strained heart." The second is the blessing poem by John O'Donohue. I share a line I love with Jean: "May there come across the waters / a path of yellow moonlight / to bring you safely home."

Poems leave her feeling uncertain, like she is once again the girl she was in high school, asked to talk about a story she didn't understand in class. Now the word *blessing* becomes a sticking point. The church, she says, must know what is going to be sent out from its pulpit. I need, she says, to submit the poems I'll read to the pastor for approval. The word *approval* bites hard, and I refuse. I want to lash out at her with *how-dare-you*'s. I want to remind her of how much she hurt him, those last months of his life, but I don't.

I have begun to see Jean in some new way I can't define yet, except that the green eyes behind her big-framed glasses seem unprotected. I see her like she is and likely has been as my father grew older. In need of a certainty aging can't provide, in need of love to assuage a loneliness that can't quite be defined. From the top of the stairs as I head to bed, I see her sitting in her recliner, holding the brown cat called Dahli. All the rooms in the house seem larger.

Upstairs, I sit on the edge of the bed while anger and grief collide inside me. I want to cry, but I can't.

* * *

When I was nine, Granddaddy had a stroke, and the message was to come quick, quick, but my mother lingered. She lingered in the bathroom at our trailer as she tried on this dress, that blouse, and slowly put on her face. She lingered in the kitchen over instant coffee and asked my father if he loved her as he stared out the window at the train tracks that led through Lynch.

What I remember most are quarrel words as we traveled from Harlan to Johnson County, trying to get to the hospital in time. I sat between them in the front seat of our Pontiac as we headed through Neon and Jenkins and all the little towns toward Paintsville. My mother lamented the late hour, our lack of a lunch. "You don't think about us a bit," she said as I felt my body sway toward her, then toward him. "What I'm thinking about is my daddy," he said. We stopped for a blue-plate special in a restaurant with a phone booth, where my father called the hospital. My granddaddy was at death's door, and my father knelt in the parking lot by our car, his face in his hands as he wept.

By the time we got to the hospital, my grandfather was in a coma, and I remember my father leading me to the bedside. "Touch him," he said. "That's what alive feels like." Later, the funeral was held in the living room at my grandparents' house. I was frightened of the crowd of people, the air smelling like sweet cake. I held my father's hand until he stood near the coffin and picked me up, showing me the body, the hands folded across the chest. "This is how it looks to die," he said. "Touch him." I did, and then I touched my father, the salt tears on his face.

* * *

Paul was as much unlike my father as possible—upper-middle class, already world traveled when I met him, and, as a good friend described him, taciturn. By the second summer of our travels, we were 7,795 miles from Kentucky, near Agra, on the banks of the Yamuna River in the Indian state of Uttar Pradesh. "Just for looking," the tour guides insisted as Paul and I were rowed across the murky waters to a hotel that had once been a palace.

By midnight, Paul was under a wet sheet to cool down to sleep. Sadness settled over me as I sat out on the balcony in the humid air, watching bats dive and arc up toward the moonlight. Sadnesses were always settling over me, and I struggled to name them. Paul and I had terminated a pregnancy so we could travel, and though I didn't want an abortion, I had acquiesced to his arguments. Neither of us make above minimum wage, he said, and when would there be another chance to travel like this? The truth was that I had long feared being pregnant, feared the shadow of my relinquished child. I hated Paul for all of it, but I loved him enough not to give him up.

A call to prayer traveled across the water from a faraway muezzin as I lie down on the smooth stone, my cheek against the cool marble. The prayer was another sadness. God hands should have scooped me up, carrying me those thousands of miles back to where I came from, the place that haunted me.

* * *

On the night before my father's service, I slip downstairs after I hear Jean go to bed. Her room is nearby, so I ease an outside door open, tiptoe in my sock feet out onto the deck. I want the sky. Clouds drift across the half-moon, and the March air is cold. I hug myself with my bare arms and send up what I hope is a demanding prayer. *The blessing is a poem about love; you know that, don't you? I loved my father, and you know that, don't you? And today. The number of dead from the virus is 3,503.* I say those numbers slowly. Say them twice, a third time, as if I am invoking a charm. The world needs one.

On the national news just this morning, some of the lost faces: An old man in a nursing home. A registered nurse at a hospital in Cleveland. A young man whose picture showed him standing on his driveway, a basketball in his hands, the whole world on the verge. On the verge of what? Falling? "Ashes, ashes." That children's rhyme catches hold inside me, and my heart thrums.

The wisps of clouds in the cold sky aren't clouds after all, I suddenly see. They are spirits. The souls of those lost so far to a virus we can't contain. Others are my ancestors—my father, my grandfather, my aunts, my mother. I stretch myself up as high as I can on my tiptoes, wishing I could make that leap, up and up and up. If I could reach the edge of the sky, just where they are floating past, I could touch them, the souls of the dead, and then. Then I might know how to cry.

"We have needed this time," Jean says, an acknowledgment that we have often shared an uneasy relationship. Days, we share meals. We watch an afternoon movie. Eat pie and ice cream. We put the finishing touches on my father's memorial and avoid talk about my father's will. Nights, I lie awake and think about the ghosts in this house.

In the mountains, ghosts are called *haints*. They are the wind down a hollow in the wintertime, howling like a woman mourning. They are caught inside the bottle tree in my front yard at home. In my father's house, the haints are politely hidden beneath the dusted shelves and sparkling floors—but they are there in the dark hall outside my bedroom. I have been uncertain whether to leave my bedroom door open or shut, since the hall seems darker and longer each night I'm there. Sometimes my father's ghost is standing in his open bedroom door, and he's waving at me. "Come listen to the story I just wrote," he's saying.

The night before his memorial, he's standing by the window in the hall, looking at the dark yard, and I know he's mourning, not just his own passing from the earth but all the other things. His loss of Jean's love. The grandson I located some years back, a young man who doesn't seem to want either of us in his life all that much. Or maybe my father is doing nothing very ghostly. He is sitting on the white and blue chair in the alcove in the hall. His ghost hands are holding a flashlight, and he's waiting for me to use the bathroom first.

* * *

On a night train from Agra to Rajasthan, was it a dream or a ghost who crept through the car, bending above each of us to unzip our bags? Paul and I lay on the filthy floor among a dozen other travelers with their sacks and backpacks. It was midsummer, and the air was thick enough to cut, so I slept in fits and starts between stations. I raised my head and watched a thin ghost man vanish into the humid air of the next station. Other ghosts haunted us. On a boat crossing the tepid waters of the Ganges, the air was as gray as ash, and I seemed to taste the ghosts of the dead. Or in that temple in Kathmandu, was it the spirit of the gods who flew over the mountaintops, whipping the prayer flags in the sharp wind? Other ghosts were small and sneaky. They crept from the mouths of strangers whose languages I did not understand except for the word that hovered in front of us. *Buy hashish. Trade money.* Sad ghosts, greedy ghosts, ghosts of gods whose faces I could not imagine. "Don't get above your raising," my father whispered across the oceans. "Don't forget who made you."

* * *

The Monday morning of the memorial, Jean and I sip coffee and watch the Home & Garden network. She is relieved, she says, that we have planned a memorial that will not go on too long. We are quiet, she and I, with things both of us want to talk about but have so far avoided. She wants to know if I have agreed to have the blessing I'll read at the memorial approved by the pastor. I want to know what loving or not loving my father meant. She wants to know what he wrote to me about those two years of their relationship's dissolution. We both want to know, after all these years, what the definition of *mother* is, the definition of *daughter*. Do those words apply to us?

The not-said is nothing new in my family, a ghost in its own right that has haunted us for generations. My maternal grandfather spent six weeks in a psychiatric ward, and we never talked about it. Never talked about the aunt who took a bottle of pills. "Just don't you mind," my mother said when I asked why they were feeding her coffee and walking her through the rooms of my grandmother's house. The list of Things Not Discussed was long. A cousin's drug abuse. Another cousin's girlfriend, rumored to have given birth to her own father's child. And my pregnancy, something that happened to another person who was not me. "What was the date my son was born?" I once asked my father. He said he could hardly remember the date of his own birth. Ghosts of hurt, secrets, surrender were inhaled like smoke, hiding in our bones and blood.

* * *

At the memorial, vials of hand sanitizer have been placed in the spot in each pew where the tiny glasses go after Communion. We are told to sit with at least six feet of distance between family groups. There is the slideshow—my father's boyhood, his air force years, a couple of photos of his marriage to my mother, my birth, glimpses of his forty-some years with Jean. While I'm watching the photos, the preacher sits in the pew ahead of me. He is young, black haired, given to blushing.

He offers his condolences and then goes right to his point. The church must know what words are going out from their pulpit. He reaches to pat my hand, and I flinch, a cold fury pouring down my back and up into my chest, filling my mouth. His approval, he says, is part of the policy of the Southern Baptist Convention and is nothing personal at all.

As the slideshow of my father ends, starts again, I am so full of the personal that I can hardly see. A woman I used to know when I was a child in this church stops beside me, offers condolences, but I can barely hear her. "Yes," I say. I say, "It's hard. Yes. I don't believe it yet." I scan the room and see Jean sitting by herself, looking at nothing. I see the faces of people I have known from years back, but I can't find the one thing, the right thing, to make this afternoon better. I can't find *it*. I'm not sure what *it* is exactly, but I know it isn't in the crowd of well-wishers, or in the lilies on the pulpit, or in the preacher's boyish face. I tell myself that this service is not about me but about my father, and I acquiesce. I hand the poems over but can hardly hear what he says, the roar in my ears is so loud.

The *it* I want is silence. Instead there are hymns. Words from the deacons, a solo about Jesus sung by a blonde-headed woman. The poems, which I read slowly and with a power that mystifies me. Then the pastor offers a prayer for my father's soul and for the end of this virus and all the other viruses that might be brought down upon us. After, as we ride the miles back to the house, I look at the lines on the palms of my hands. I check Google on my phone and look up the names of some of the lines. *Life. Marriage. Health. Heart.* I am not sure which the correct line for grieving is.

* * *

My family holds on to grief. My paternal grandmother, once my grandfather passed, held her grieving close and never married again. "He always said there's all kinds of men out there," she told me. My mother, once my parents divorced, moved back in with her own parents and lived there for good. The refrain she repeated again and again: "You know your father should have treated us better." Closets in my mother's house held letters, clothes, knickknacks, photos of the dead. The loss of my son traveled with me everywhere I went until I wrote a memoir, named my own grief. My father's sorrows went unnamed for the most part. Did he mourn the marriage he couldn't sustain with my mother? The grandson he never got to know? The changed nature of Jean's love? I remember his hands, the bitten nails and cuticles, the signs of hurt he carried wherever he went.

* * *

My furtive sleep entwined with Paul's as we lay next to each other in a beat-up tent with vinyl ponchos for a covering against the rain that fell in Ireland and England, Switzerland and France. We learned we no longer loved each other, no longer wanted touch or shared breath or histories. I resented him for not listening, and he resented me for telling the same stories about unresolved hurt again and again. Still, we traveled. Overland via bus through Yugoslavia. Greece. Thailand. In Australia, we climbed Uluru and looked out over a sea of red earth, our arms draped across each other's shoulders.

My father wrote me letters about our plans to travel on to India: "When we think of Asia, we think of bad places." I sent postcards back home, ones with photos of elephants with hennaed bindi between their eyes. In Delhi, we prayed for a breeze to cool our separate bodies in the premonsoon listlessness. Which grief to write about and send back home—this one, this one, this?

* * *

On the Tuesday after the memorial service, Jean and my cousin Chris and I drive to eastern Kentucky to scatter my father's ashes at Dewey Lake, near Prestonsburg. I sit in the back seat, holding on to the box that holds my father's ashes. We are quiet for our ride, listening to soft rock from the radio in Jean's car. I offer up bits and pieces of the news to Chris, whom I have not seen in years. The administration has known about this virus since January, I say. Today's death count is 7,087.

Atop my knees is the box for my father's ashes. I hold it close as we take Route 302 into Jenny Wiley, the State Resort Park. We pass the cottages and then May Lodge, where we stop at the information desk. "Where would the best place be to sit and then scatter ashes?" Arrowhead Point is a ten-minute drive around the lake and then a quick walk out to a spot that would be just right. We head east alongside the lake, then find ourselves at a rocky projection of land. I hold tightly to the box as we leave the car and make our way down a gradual incline. Holding on to the box gives me gravity. It's like that ritual in the churches I went to when I was small. *Laying on hands.* Laying on hands meant feeling the Holy Spirit as it coursed beneath someone else's skin. It meant healing.

I imagine my father walking with us. He's saying nothing much: "Maybe the rain will hold off. I thought there'd be an observation deck." Jean is following me, picking her way gingerly on flat stones slick with mud, my cousin Chris behind her as we descend a last rocky incline. The lake water is late-winter muddy, a dull surface with no visible bottom. It's hard to see the reason we picked this spot—the photos we've all seen of my father as a boy, swimming at Dewey Lake with his brother.

Jean and I hold the box between us, picking at the packing tape, arriving at the plastic sack inside. Jean, Chris, and I pass the sack from one to the next and scatter the ashes, little by little. "Here's to forty-seven years, Clarence," Jean says. I read a Wendell Berry poem. Chris stands a long while, saying nothing. Soon the bag is empty of the final offerings we each have to give.

* * *

A *Washington Post* article from late April 2020 says that we must find new ways to mourn. By May, the virus will have claimed over eighty thousand lives in the United States and well over four million globally. There are so many ways of mourning. The Caribbean Nine Nights of feasting, singing, and storytelling. The Muslim three-day remembrance. The weeklong Jewish practice of sitting shiva. My own people's custom of visitation and a funeral in the home. But what is it we are grieving? Are we grieving the six feet of distance between ourselves and everyone else? Am I grieving the kind of fear I feel as I walk up the sidewalk past a group of men working, fearing not their catcalls but their lack of masks? Are we grieving the new divides? The fortunates. The remotes. The essential workers. All the rest.

Faces are what I continue to mourn as weeks turn to the months of a pandemic. On the front page of a local paper, I see the face of a mother who has contracted the virus and cannot see her newborn. I see the face of a ninety-year-old man who has miraculously survived contagion but can see his family only through a glass wall. All of us are grieving. Grieving this house, that house, this person, people infinitum, all connected by virtual images, not touch. We are grieving a world that used to be, this world become one of tenuous intimacies. If we wear them, our masks cover our mouths, leaving our words muffled, our eyes not quite saying what we really mean.

* * *

Once Paul and I were back home again, things went further south, with love affairs and distance, emotional exhaustion. Finally, Paul was the one to do the leaving. I no longer loved him, but I grieved fiercely and wanted it all back again, him and our travels, our beat-up tent, and all the nights of rain. I visited a nave in a chapel in North Carolina to see a painting of the Holy Mother, her son in her arms, the wounds in his side and hands and head spilling blood on her white robes. *Pleasepleaseplease*, I prayed, staring into Mary's blue-painted eyes. What was I praying for? Paul, magically returned, voilà, my savior from deeper hurts I scarcely understood? My son, descending from the sky, a baby all over again? Some days I was scarcely able to get out of bed. One night I had a dream of myself lying flat on my stomach on the sofa, head hanging over the floor. A map of the world was below me, one made of tears turned to ice. Finally, the sadness passed.

In the years after that, I traveled again, to graduate school, then on to years of teaching in Georgia, West Virginia, South Dakota, state upon state. "Don't wait too long to get you a home," my father said as I moved again and again for teaching jobs and writer's residencies. I married my partner, John, put down roots. We bought a house in Maryland, planted a garden. I wrote books. "I suppose I'd say you're unethical," my father said when he read the memoir I'd written about the surrender of my son to adoption. Then he gave the book to friends, underlined passages as he read it over and over. "You got that wrong," he'd say. "I was in Morocco in 1954, not in Korea." On my many visits home, we sat with each other, both of us fumbling for the right thing to say, the one thing to absolve both of us from wounds for which we had no words.

* * *

I was six the morning after my parents fought all night long, their voices raw. My father drove me to school, his face flushed as he pushed the gas pedal down, raced us along the two-lane until I began to cry. Then he pulled over at a grassy place. "Forgive me," he said. "None of it will ever happen again." Of course, he was wrong. There were other times they argued, long and fiercely. There were other cars and other highways, even if the driver was not my father. And there are so many other times and gestures and actions I have regretted. The children I've never had. The towns I've left behind, taking road after road. The search for this place, that one, seeking reparation. How far I've traveled, looking for the ability to trust, for openness to love.

My father had his own journeys. What he'd have thought of this time of the pandemic, I can guess. Fear. Faith. A mixture of the two he'd have drunk like a cure. In the year before he died, he wrote to me again and again, long emails about aging, about decisions he could never change. There are vows we take, he said, and he wrote to me about his marriages, the grandson he'd never known, the absolute belief he professed in God. I think of the trail of his ashes as we scattered them. There's no telling where the waters took him or how far.

WE WERE ALL SOMETHING ONCE

It's April 2020, the long weeks of quarantine, and I have been taking walks every morning with my dog. The trail that used to be for a trolley in Ellicott City has waterfalls and cliffsides. In a large patch of woods, there are deer, a skinny red fox, and the half-burned remains of a large house covered in graffiti. There's a hill I climb, overlooking my neighborhood. I stand looking down at houses with chimneys trailing smoke. A yard with a chicken coop and goats. Children are tumbling head over heels down a grassy incline.

* * *

Another time, another incline.

I was five.

My parents took me to a church celebration. Punch and cake. Easter eggs in the flower beds. The children set free to play.

Stomach, back, stomach, I rolled all the way to the bottom of an incline, where I lay looking up at my mother. She was standing against the skyline, her face angry, her mouth a red-lipsticked *O*. Her spiky heels sank into the moist earth as she inched her way down. "Just look," she said. "You're filthy." She slapped me, quick and clean.

* * *

Memoir, essayist Patricia Hampl says, "is real, tangible, made of the stuff of a life lived in place and in history." I remember the sensation of my body turning and turning. Grassy scent of the hill. Sting of hand on face.

Memoir tells us how things looked, gives us a sense of who said what and when. With memoir, we remember the hardest places and words, the most difficult lacks and losses. With memoir, we become accountable.

Do I remember in order to let go of this past? If we remember, do we forgive?

* * *

Late May, and my dog nudges me to walk, walk, but I am heavy with grief. Three million worldwide have been infected with COVID-19, and nearly one hundred thousand Americans have died. Those losses slam hard against my own. A year ago in March, my mother passed away, and my father died this February. The air tastes like sorrow.

I walk until my legs remember how, and I count beautiful things. Lilac. A crow's call. Spiderwebs in clear sunlight. I have lost myself in seeing until, on the hill overlooking the neighborhood, it happens.

Memory picks me up by the scruff of my neck. "Listen here," it says and shakes me until spring rewinds.

Seed pods unsprout, and the wind inhales. Red petals draw their thin tongues in while the songs of birds fly back inside their mouths. The world in reverse is frightening and glorious.

I am fifty. Forty. Twenty.

I am five and lying at the bottom of a green, green hill with some other children, our mouths full of laughter. My mother is standing over me, her mouth unfrowning. Her hand pulls back from my face, the fingers trailing along my skin. "Just look," she says. I watch as she unclimbs, her high heels unsticking from the ground, carrying her back to where she began.

* * *

From Patricia Hampl's essay "Memory and Imagination": "The authority of memory is a personal confirmation of selfhood. To write one's life is to live it twice, and the second living is both spiritual and historical."

My mother's authority was mementos. Tarnished silver candy dish. China dogs on a chain. Photo of me when I was twelve. Old leather handbag filled with letters and photos.

Second living was not something she chose. She chose bitterness over love, guarded her losses jealously. Then she dived straight into Alzheimer's forgetting, and history became random sentences, phrases, then no words at all.

* * *

The virus, they say, began with bats. Bats in a jungle with no name in the center of the world. A bat clinging to damp clay on the ceiling of a cave. Flexing its wings and claws, licking its teeth. Sipping darkness, a sweet Madeira. It opens its mouth and hisses, its belly fat with possibility, but then it too remembers some other time. Bats were sacred then. *Sacred.* A word that means nothing now. A bat clings to damp clay, opens its mouth, and inhales. Takes the fear back inside. What could have been born digests and disappears. Like this, the world ungrieves.

* * *

Perhaps what we do with writing memoir is circle the wagons. Shore up an overflowing pond of memory with sandbags. Or maybe we're walking a maze, over and over and over, until we are closer to the center of ourselves.

* * *

Consider a black-and-white photograph. My mother is fourteen years old in this photo, and she is standing with her mother, father, and sister Ruby, just outside a church house door. My grandfather, called Pa, is wearing a short-sleeved shirt, and he is standing sideways with his arm outstretched, holding the door open. There is darkness behind him—a shadowed hall or room. My grandmother is standing to one side of that door, arm folded over arm. She is much shorter than Pa, diminished by him. She is neither smiling nor not, a gold tooth glinting. Two girls, my mother-to-be, Pearlie, and my aunt Ruby. Ruby's hand is resting against her mouth, and Pearlie is holding the hem of her dress to either side of her.

Behind this photograph is another one made of history.

My mother was raised poor. Five-room house, no electricity, no room for privacy, outhouse down the hill. My granny's life was working in the garden, cooking, using a wringer washer. Pa worked the deep mines, home dead tired by dark, ready to pray. Later on, when the girls began to date, he met their beaux with a shotgun. I imagine him hoarding the love of his wife, his girls, his son, saving it for himself.

Sometimes I enter that photograph. Duck underneath his arm, step inside a room. The room is in a house, though it is not God's. The room is a bedroom where all six of them sleep, and my mother loves to slip in there in the afternoons when her siblings are out. My granny is plucking the ripest tomatoes to slice up for supper. The house is quiet.

She's washed her hair with rain and an auburn rinse, and she lifts a hand mirror, takes a look at the finger curls. She studies her face. Brows thin enough? Teeth white against the red? Wipe the lipstick off. It's five o'clock, and Pa will be home soon.

Later, she'll tiptoe through the kitchen and out the back door. Yes, that boy. He'll meet her at the bottom of the hill below the house, him in that car with its big back seat. What will a kiss feel like? She is lost in wishing, and she almost doesn't notice. Pa is standing in the doorway, filling it up with the soot black of his work clothes, the scent of his sweat. In his face is a desire she doesn't know how to name, a rage that makes her cower.

What I have is a photograph.

Pa's smile is a hitch to the side of his mouth, an offhand smile that dismisses. The body is upright, eyes mocking. They meet the gaze of the photographer. He is caught forever, holding the door open, the muscles in his short-sleeved shirt ropy and strong looking, his arm barring the door.

MNEMOSYNE

A minor goddess, described as one of the three original Muses in Greek mythology. Mnemosyne is often the patron goddess of poetry, the goddess of time and memory. Her priestesses were taught to drink from the river of memory, to possess the power of the soul. Mnemosyne, a kind of mother of the past.

* * *

I am twelve.

I am lying in a bathtub full of water, my legs spread.

Raise up, my mother says, and I do.

She lathers the soap with her hands and touches my body. My pubic hair has not blossomed. My breasts are barely formed. I have begun to menstruate, but my mother calls that *a curse*.

She tells me how it will be to become a woman. How I'll take the first boy who'll have me. "Being a woman," she says as she washes me, "is nothing but trouble."

I stand on a towel while she dries me off, and from there I can see both of us in the full-length mirror on the bathroom door. I hold my legs out one by one for the towel. She kneels in front of me, drying, drying, her body tense. Forehead wrinkled, green eyes narrowed, she is angry, but I am not sure at whom. Me, because I was born?

I have held on to this memory all my life. I have made a photo of it to study. Nurtured this memory until it is full-blown, sotted with its own power.

I have written this memory over and over, in poems, essays, fiction. What I can never completely do is go back to the room.

Back to the mirror.

Back to her hand, raised to her lips.

Back to her father's face and his rage.

Inside memory, rage and desire hang in the air like a toxic scent she breathes in.

If my mother had known how to name such things, would everything that came afterward have been different?

* * *

My memory hands touch my mother's face in the mirror. Fingers outline the perfect red of her mouth.

Like this, I can do anything.

I can make her smile.

Make the rage on his face unwind like the metal coil inside a watch.

Make every night full of explicable shadows.

Make the smile become a song, become years, become me.

Outside the bathroom door, she hands me the clothes she has just washed for me and soap that smells like flowers.

I shut the door, and inside that room, my body is a secret neither of us knows.

Water rushes into the tub, and I step inside.

* * *

By the middle of June, the world is burning. There are 385,000 dead worldwide. Thousands protest racial injustice in cities across the globe. Minneapolis. Houston. London. Amsterdam. Berlin. Auckland. Words echo on social media: *"I can't breathe."* Laying my hands on the keyboard, I seem to feel the power of rage, distilled. I tell myself the world is better than this. Inhale through my nose, exhale through my mouth. I say it again and again and again. *Breathe. Breathe. Breathe.* The world is a colorless slate.

It is made of shattered glass.

The metaphors. The only way is to mix them.

The only way is to remember it. A world where air is sweet, unbreathed. The only way is to push words out from the throat. Make the world begin again.

* * *

"The down side of any created thing," says Patricia Hampl, is that we "must live with a version that attaches us to our limitations, to the inevitable subjectivity, of our points of view. We must acquiesce to our experiences and our gift to transform experience into meaning and value."

My mother died on March 9, 2019.

She lived for almost fifty years in her parents' house in Lancer, Kentucky, lived daily with all the untreated symptoms of an obsessive-compulsive personality. Clean hands. Clean floors. A whole life built on the immaculate.

And then she dived.

Dived into bowls of pudding until she could no longer use a spoon. Dived into a sleep she never left.

And me?

Is the death of a parent also the death of the quintessential moment?

Presto! Hurt becomes strength.

Becomes experience.

Voilà! Violation is transformed.

And then this. How to forgive? Forget? Surrender?

Language does not always seem infinite.

* * *

Another morning toward the end of June. Pandemic numbers have not been consistent these last couple of weeks. On one site, I see 2,424,565 listed as the number of those in the United States infected by COVID-19. A news article has this subtitle: "I Will Not Wear a Mask to Protect Your Health. I Don't Wear It to Protect My Civil Liberties." A post on social media lists four reasons to wear a mask. "I would rather," the post says, "do all I can to help slow the spread (even if it's determined later that such protections were not needed) than to do less and cause harm."

My dog and I take our morning rambles farther. I wear my mask, but I try to go where there's no one. Walks at 6:00 a.m.

I've also ventured into a wood on the outskirts of one of my habitual streets. First, we went only to a clearing full of ferns, then on to a metal-fenced-in area, the concrete lush with gigantic mullein plants.

Another day we arrived at the remains of a mansion, its third floor charred by fire, its first floor with doors wide open. Just inside, a trash-filled indoor pool. Abundant graffiti. "Make Me Sad. We Were All Something Once. God Isn't Coming Back." The place was once elegant, with its glassed-in roof, now broken, above the pool. The marble counters in a kitchen with the cabinets now ripped off the walls. The house is all crash and burn and broken now.

* * *

On my third week of visits to the abandoned mansion, I toss out all precautions and make my way up to the second floor:

Anything is possible in that room. Dancing and raging fun. Freebasing by the fireplace. An ordinary apocalypse.

I let the dog sniff while I explore. A closet with one beat-up coat hanging from a singed cloth-covered hanger. An empty box. A nightstand with half a letter, written in pencil: "Bae, you no I luv u." Then I sit down on the edge of the bed. The dog sniffs at the edge of the smoked carpet and then leaps up onto the filthy coverlet.

Long enough for me to bask in it.

A scent of ash and smoke that will linger in my hair. Sunlight through the broken window. The room's ghosts of frivolity. *Red. Green. Blue.* All the colors of some night before, and the bed, too, its memories of bodies from before, and before that, and before that.

Who am I in such a world made of suffering?

Do I have a choice?

* * *

She says:

"I drink from the river of memory."

"Like this I have a soul."

* * *

News articles predict that the world will never be the same.

There are the numbers. They will flatten, and soon, it is hoped, a cure will be discovered. Some claim that the United States should have more than a hundred million doses of a potential vaccine by early 2021. Others are less optimistic and acknowledge that accurate insight into anything as complex as the COVID-19 pandemic, no less a feasible date for a vaccine, is the stuff of science fiction. Science is crucial, and hope is absolutely necessary. A vaccine might indeed be sent down to us on a beam of light from a darkening sky.

How can the world ever be the same, its embraces, its breaths freely taken?

I imagine that.

Breath. One breath. An enormous breath in from the earth and back out to the sky, out to the blackness of space where nothing, we think, exists. All those insidious droplets, and along with them, all our fears and reckonings, our enormous grief, sent into an airless cosmic place most of us will never see. The still-animate virus, breathed out, coasting along in deep space with no known destination, winding its way past asteroids and planets, nameless stars and galaxies, whole undiscovered populations. And us? Free again to travel, make love, cavort even.

Time rewound, before the infection, before the quintessential harm.

It could all be so easy.

Some days I think in terms of ease, of unremembering, on a smaller scale. My mother, back from dying, up from her deathbed, memory washing through her blood, revitalizing her cells. She could walk back, year upon year.

Along the way, she could revisit me, relove me, and I her, forgiveness no longer necessary.

Memoir, as the essayist says, is a second living . . . reaching deep within. Deep within? Hearts. Subcellular selves. The secrets inside us, given a second chance.

It could be.

* * *

A world where air is sweet, unbreathed.

Push the words out from the throat.

Begin again.

ANIMALS

WOLVES

We'd been on the road for almost two years—hitchhiking, doing agricultural work, restaurant work—anything we could get to take us from country to country to country. After our return, we live in the farmhouse our friend Saury rents. We'd left our dog and everything we owned with him, pretravels. The farm itself is ten thousand rolling acres owned by New Yorkers with investments in South African diamond mines. Pond, orchard, beef cattle. Cattle roam behind neat white fences, and deer leap barbed wire into the tangle of woods on the farm's perimeters.

I talk to Saury some nights when I can't sleep. He is practical and well-versed in jazz. He tells me that Miles Davis was a shy man. He tells me how to fan rice as it cooks. He tells me how his wife left him and now spends most of her time alone in her apartment with a telemarketing job. I tell him travel tales. Trains, buses. The Taj Mahal. That beggar in a puppeteer's booth in India, his missing fingers. We sit by the woodstove until there's nothing to tell, and then I slip into the fingers of moonlight in our room.

The ten thousand acres are covered in snow, and I huddle near your long limbs, still thinking about India. That bus ride to a national park to see tigers. An elephant ride into a jungle. There were no tigers that day, but I remember climbing up the steep side of the elephant, sitting on top of her, only for her to refuse to walk once we were seated. An Indian guide slammed a sharp metal prod into her side again and again. In my memory you say, "What do you want me to do about it?" When I finally sleep, I dream I am in the mountains. I am walking, walking so far north there are only deep forests and the howls of wolves.

THE *OXFORD ENGLISH DICTIONARY* DEFINITIONS OF *DESIRE*:

(a) To long for; to want earnestly, as he who desires the pelt of a wolverine. (b) In Homer: *thumos*, used to denote emotions, desire, or an internal urge; when a Homeric hero is under emotional stress, he may externalize his thumos and converse with or scold it. (c) To express a wish for—e.g., Edmund Spenser, "a doleful case desires a doleful song." (d) To request the presence or attendance of something, as in Shakespeare, "A horse, a horse! My kingdom for a horse!" (e) To entreat or demand; to command (Percy Bysshe Shelley): "Rise like Lions after slumber / in unvanquishable number—Shake your chains to earth like dew."

MONKEY DREAMS

I need the quiet of the farm to write my travel stories, ones with camels hissing and hot wind blowing across the deserts of Rajasthan. I sit upstairs with my notebook, leaving the windows open wide. I hear cows crying across the road, mothers whose calves have been taken for sale. As September becomes October, I start spending most of my time in the upstairs rooms, while you inhabit the downstairs. I hear work boots tread from kitchen to living room to outside where you split logs for kindling in the leaf-strewn yard. When the room grows warm, I nap on a twin bed, sleeping fitfully. One dream becomes another. Wild-eyed monkeys on the walls of abandoned temples become women in red saris on the steps of an abandoned temple. And that child we aborted. In dreams she is a wild animal, a primal cry that wakes me again and again.

HEAT

In Delhi, we slept on a rooftop and listened as a fight broke out in the street. In Jaipur, rabid dogs bared their teeth and growled in the dark. In Santorini, it was so hot the inside of the tent sweated with the condensation of our breath. On the Great Barrier Reef, I snorkeled far out into the hot blue sea, unable without my glasses to see the splendors of sea turtles. We slept naked in bed after bed in place after place in the summer's blaze. It was too hot to touch. Desire could not transcend heat.

A WOMAN DEFINES *DESIRE*

(a) To want the moon to remain perfect and still. (b) To dream of a map and of swimming and swimming and never reaching the far shore. (c) Piano music and a light beneath a closed door. (d) Fire, fire inside, and the coolness of a lover's touch. (e) To ask, ask. Silence. (f) To slip outside naked and reach hard for the stars spinning in the hot sky. (g) To drink cool clear water that tastes like sadness. (h) A blank page followed by another blank page. (i) The sound of foxes, more human than us.

CATTLE

Sometimes I think I never wanted you but all the places you'd been before me. A kibbutz in Israel. Floating on a blanket on the salt of the Dead Sea. That woman in France, how you stood in an alley with her, raised her skirt and how your bodies moved against a doorway. Seas and mountains. Deserts and city streets. Beds with netting and gardens that smelled of frangipani. I take you in my mouth and feel the soft skin of you on my tongue, the imagined distances growing farther and farther away. Cattle moan at night from the field, and the sound is a taste in my throat. The soles of my feet tingle, as though I could run miles in my sleep.

FALSE SPRING

At night, there's the scent of foxes from open windows. I feel life stirring in my throat and lie thinking of your generous mouth, your wet tongue. It's as if I've never touched you before, your belly and the soft line of hair traveling down, parting at your thighs. I tug until you are awake. We haven't made love in weeks and weeks, have slept in the closed-down spaces of our separate bodies. I sit up, lift the tee shirt away from my body. You are partly naked in the shadowy room, and then there is a scent I do not remember as you. This is the scent of winter and rooms too cold for showers. It is the scent of forgotten desire. You reach for me, stopping my hands mid-want. It's been weeks, you say, and it's true. It's true how far the winter has to go.

SPRING

We sometimes let the dog out at the start of the mile-long road to the farmhouse, and she runs and runs, her body alight, her delighted tongue lolling. Other times we spend an hour sitting in the car, dog in the back seat as we argue. You tell me I don't know how to see abundance. *Red. Gold. Green. Blue. Amber.* The colors in the greenhouses each spring. You say I don't know how to be happy, and I say that I was happy once, though I do not say it was with you. I want to tell you how much it would mean if on the road to the house we took the curve to the right rather than the left, ended up in the field on the other side of the pond. We could step out of our shoes, discard everything, see the sunset across our naked bodies. One finger could trace a line beginning at the side of an eye, under a nose, down the center of a chest. Before I can describe any of it, I realize that the body I am imagining is not yours at all. Your body is an absence, an empty. You are right. Happiness is a language I don't know, one I have left beside some road in a country with a name I no longer remember. I say I'll walk back, and I open the car door as the dog jumps out beside me, her body quivering with eagerness.

COLORS

France was the slick purple skins of grapes we harvested and succulent beef tongue on a platter at noon. Switzerland was clear ice and the silver bells of goats. Yugoslavia was the black scarf covering a woman's head as she cut off the chicken's head and then made our soup. Santorini was azure and white. Singapore was the yellow and blue of feathers in a park for exotic birds. Rajasthan was red and gold and camels in a blaze of heat. Thailand was the cool gray and green of a peacock feather fan across the temple floors. I breathed all the colors deep inside and have never known how to let them go.

MOON'S YELLOW EYE

I love night runs, my shadow trailing me along the asphalt. A great horned owl fans its wings and settles in the boughs of a giant oak, preens itself as it looks for night prey. The night is made of claw sounds, cicada sounds, breath sounds from my chest. Soon I've run two miles up the road from the house, and I pause at the bend where pasture meets road. There are two adjoining greenhouses full of starts of spring plants, and I walk over there, spread my fingers against a glassed-in door, peer inside.

Inside, long benches with soil-filled flats. My skin is warm from running, then cool in the chill, dirt-smelling air. I sit on a bench, pull my knees into my arms. I have worked here for a couple of springs, checks that help pay my way in the classes I take in creative writing. I wait as the ghosts of the ladies from last spring drift from bins of soil to flats. Their shapes bend and lift in the dark, float from bench to bench, float above me, laughing.

Other ghosts make their way, one by one, through the moist, humus-scented air. Ghost of a black bear I once saw on the other side of the pond. Groundhog ghost that nosed into the compost at the back of the house. Dog ghost, home from a night away in the woods, a scrap of fur in her mouth. You ghost, your arms full of empty pots to fill with soil, your face pleased with how red the blossoms will be, how orange, how white, how violet. Me ghost, my head full of words, lifts her hands, trying to catch words before they drift down and disappear. Your ghost pauses, then lifts from the greenhouse floor, floats out into the huge night. A fox barks and a wisp of tail vanishes toward the mountains. The ragged sound of my breath as I run and run and run.

DOG

Yellow, purple, and orange are the colors of the blooms in autumn, but I am not there. I have jumped ship. Left you and the dog and the roommate and the farmhouse. Slipped off into the sunset. Headed off to a place where writers write and learn their craft. Where writers drink and dance and eat waffles at dawn at a diner downtown in a southern city I've come to love more than I love you. I visit you some weekends, and Saury makes omelets as light as air. The three of us eat and sip wine and listen to jazz, and the dog looks at me with eyes full of hurt. Soon I am south again, writing and studying books.

TELEPHONE BAR

One night I am in a telephone bar, which means each table has an old-fashioned phone so you can call someone you want to flirt with.

I am calling a man with a baseball cap on backward at the next table. He's a man with a big laugh, a man with fine black hairs on his one finger. He's in the writing program I've joined, and he writes stories about Alaska and working at a fishery, about a tattooed stripper, about a bag of cocaine blown away in a windstorm. He is a man I want, but I have not yet acted on this. You come to visit me in the southern city, and you walk with me in the flea market, buy me an antique jewelry box painted with Japanese water lilies, and I think, oh, yes, that is why I love you, but I do not, no matter how hard I try. When I sleep next to you in my rented room, you lie along my body like it is a familiar country, but that's a lie. Where I am is in another country altogether. I'm flirting in a telephone bar with a man not you, and my heart skitters and skips.

Soon I don't call you on the weekends, don't send you postcards, don't visit you at all, except for once in later October, when you and Saury welcome me home with a big pan of spicy chicken and rice. We lie in the dark watching murder mysteries on a small black-and-white television, and you try to touch me, but I turn over, sleep hard. After that visit, the dog travels with me to the southern city, but I am distracted, pacing instead of dog walking. The dog looks at me with hungry eyes, and I realize that neither of us has eaten. I am spinning, weaving. The ground beneath my feet is opening, and I am ready to fall inside, and the fall, I know, will be delicious.

On a Saturday night, I take the dog and drive to the place where the baseball-capped man is house-sitting for one of our writing mentors. It's a fine white house, with a big porch and a garden with a marble table where we sit, sipping whiskey. There's a fire in a fire pit, and the dog paces, wondering where she is. Wondering, maybe, where you are, but I tell her to sit and keep her on a short leash as we take a walk down the country road.

It's chilly out, but we have our glasses of whiskey, ice tinkling as we pass leafless trees. For weeks we have been thinking about becoming lovers, but now that D-Day is here, I'm wary. It's not so much, I tell myself, that I will be unfaithful. What does that mean, after all? It's been almost four years now with you, and what we've become is the memory of other places. What we've become is a shovel and rake, the turn of black soil in a pot. We've become friends, not lovers, and this man in his baseball cap? Desire shivers inside me as I rattle the ice in my glass.

We walk a half mile up the road, stop to sip our drinks, stop to touch hands, kiss. We've kissed before, by bar light, at midnight after readings, and again at the foot of the South's most enormous star at a viewing point above the city. We walk, and the light is getting late-fall thinner, and we stop again, thinking of heading back. The evening will stretch ahead of us with more drinks, with They Might Be Giants playing on a boom box and us dancing until we sweat, our mouths tasting of cigarettes. But just then the dog raises her snout and howls. In the road ahead of us, a shape flaps as we inch forward. A green-feathered turkey lies there, eyes wild. It is part alive, part broken winged, and the dog sniffs excitedly.

My soon-to-be lover sets his cap back farther on his head, urges me to head on back. Soon I'll shed my clothes like an unwanted skin, and he will touch me with his black-haired finger until I come, as if I am surprised, as if I've never been that alive. Now I inch along the road, the dog's leash in hand, watching as this lover kneels, picks the turkey up, and snaps its neck, a clean, quick break.

HOWLING AT THE MOON

Lean young man with his long hair tied back, gold etched around his front teeth, his room filled with oil paintings I don't necessarily like. Another painter, at a retreat where I'm working on a novel. His paintings are fabulous. Red. Gold leaf. I try to make narratives from these paintings as we make love and then lie talking on a mattress on the floor. Then there's a writer from an English department where I teach part-time. I meet him at his house up a holler where shadows arrive at five. There's a pixie-haired woman who takes me to diners and holds my hand and cuddles with me in a king-size bed. A muscle-armed country guy with a red car who comes to my driveway to fix a water pump. The artist who pours four inches of vodka into a glass and tosses it back while his hands shake as he shows me his sketches. Lovers become a chant in my heart. Lovers before you leave me. Lovers before I had the guts to leave you. All the lovers after. In my dreams, their faces are as interchangeable as clouds. I take out those memory lovers one by one, questioning what I felt when, what I felt where, whether I felt anything in particular, anything at all.

CRAZY QUILT

Shadow of a plane moving forward. Climbed mountains and the valleys beyond and beyond and the scent of oak as it splits. The yellow-tailed hornet that stings my right hand at the greenhouse; how you do not stop working long enough to look? Drip of sap from a tapped tree in the yard, but not enough for syrup. The dog, howling at nothing. Half a sweater I never finish knitting. The motion of a ferry boat that rocks us to sleep. Your hand holding mine as we cross a busy street. Two years of countries. Waves of heat rising from a desert. Giant turtle's fingers undulating in the sea. Your mouth, which I want to like kissing. A mile of poinsettias and the tepid greenhouse air. A red so rich it wants to come off on my hands. "Touch me like this," I say, and I show you where, but you say, okay, okay, while I close my eyes and imagine the fingers are not mine, not yours. Rickety bridge that crosses a river and the way my heart stops as I follow you. Planes and buses and our own two feet and then a farmhouse in the country and a wild, beating heart. Traveling with no destination. How you move across my body quick, quick, the final exhale in my ears. Taste of an avocado plucked from the branch of a tree. Deer panting and your hands, gently untangling her from the barbed wire she tried to leap. I wish that all the fragments could find an order, but there is no order. There is a story with no end.

ABACUS

Thirty years later, I will track you down on an internet site. You are an accountant these days, and I say, oh, of course. I remember you standing by a boat in Kashmir, bargaining with the man who got angry and abandoned us at dusk across a huge lake. Us, changing money in a blazing-hot street, and you counting, counting every rupee. That weeping ficus you brought home, nurtured back to life. Did I realize how much it retailed for? I see you bent over a desk, an old-fashioned ledger opened in front of you, your hands in fingerless gloves. You are tallying, tallying. You blow a candle out. The memories go dark.

CONCATENATION

West. East. Lost, found. I have finally dived deep into a life I've made with a man who is my partner, my companion. John, a good man who I love with all of me. A Monacan from Virginia. A man who has made peace with his own life. Soon after we first met, he knocked on my door in the middle of the night, his clothes with the scent of sage smoke. "Where have you been?" I asked. I held him as he told me about how he'd been lighting sage over the remains of his ancestors, returned, hard won, from ownership by state museums. He is a man of honor. He has made my whole self catch fire with the curiosity of his hands, his mouth, his stories.

Still, I hear about you sometimes in notes from friends. "He is sealed off, rusty in conversing. He can't let himself out." I can't entirely let you out either. Ghost you. Memory you. I remember the Indian guide, the sharp metal prod slamming into that elephant's side, and you saying, "What can I do about it?" Tears filled your eyes as you stroked the rough and tender elephant skin, a tenderness I was not capable of seeing.

There are ghosts of you inside me. The sound of your footsteps on a screened-in porch. Sound of a whistle in the dark, calling our dog to come on home. Scent of sweat on a bare chest. Hair on your arms made gold by the hot sun. How beautiful you were. The scent of loam and work. My bare breasts against you as we settled into the grass. Your face as we sat in the yard after. You, your blue shirt unbuttoned. These years and years later, desire is the memory of a space beneath a door, a shadow moving away. A scatter of moths against a lit globe and two beings lying on a bed, so close they could touch, so close they do not.

LEAVING

July 27, 2022, Baltimore County. It's 3:00 a.m., and I've been awake reading since midnight, reading about the heavy rain in Kentucky. Between July 25 and 29, rains and flash flooding and river flooding stretched across fourteen eastern Kentucky counties. Hundreds of homes would be destroyed, forty-five people killed, and hundreds of families displaced. This night I remember other floods when I was a child. Water to the top of our Pontiac's hubcaps as we drove through a town called Neon. Water to the upstairs apartment where my grandparents once lived in Allen. And a story I used to hear about a flood and an ancestor who lived near Dwale, the little place my mother's people were from. *Killed by a rock big as a house,* they'd say. No name for this woman ancestor has come down to me, so I've taken a name for her from family history. I have called her Nethaladia.

I imagine Nethaladia during days of rain and more rain. Maybe it was twilight when she heard it, a deep itch and rumble as she stood by the hill. Not quite a sound and not a living thing, but it moved from the top of that hill and took hold inside her, moved from her heart to her throat. There was a wet give and moan, a flush of earth and rocks and roots tearing free. She'd somehow dreamed such a thing many a time, how the earth could open up on a whim, make a giant hole into forever that could swallow the house and her and all the freedom for which she'd secretly begged. This sound was less earth than mountain, more mountain than her own self. A giant stone falls from the mountain's top, tumbles down heedless as rain. A slow moment gaining speed, headed for the space where she'd so often stood, taking time to dream.

***

Nethaladia. Exer. Het. Hermentia. Beck. Della. Their names spill from my mouth, a homily, though I'm not completely certain which women were which. I took trips back to eastern Kentucky trying to look up courthouse records about who lived when. I inherited a book from my father, a county history from my father's people in Johnson County. I talked with relatives and friends of relatives. My mother's people in Floyd County have no written history, though they claim a colorful history that includes the outlaw Belle Star. From them I have inherited pictures and letters, my mother's wedding rings, an autographed high school yearbook.

My father, a natural born storyteller, gave me the legends I have tucked away. There was the Bearded Lady, a great-great-grandmother—a woman who traveled with a carnival. There was the great-grandmother who married at thirteen, young enough to sit on the floor and play with her first child's doll babies like they were her own. My mother's stories were speculation about who had done what and gone where. There was Nethaladia. There was the aunt who ran away to be a go-go dancer. There was a madwoman in an attic. There were the names of cities where this one or that one had gone, once upon a time. *Indianapolis. Akron. Detroit.* Foreign countries where people went and often never came back.

I take up these stories and make of them a many-colored quilt, one with my favorite pattern, Trip around the World. Around a central square, an artist sews journey after journey, trip after trip. The quilt I imagine is made of women ancestors who dream of journeys. Escape into a city. Escape into imagination. Escape unto death. If I don't know the exact dimensions of these journeys—the tickets they bought, the miles they drove, or the extent of their imaginings—I believe I understand that desire for flight.

***

Devastation is not new for the eastern Kentucky I have known since I was a child. Mining has meant deep damage—cropland and forests become pits and quarries, soil left porous, and runoff turned to flooding. Mine wastes are mind-blowing—tens of millions of tons per year, including solid waste from the mines, refuse from coal washing and preparation, and sludge from treating acid mines. Mines damage ecosystems, and the power plants associated with mining emit large quantities of carbon dioxide. The health impacts range from cancer to damage to the nervous and immune systems. Environmental effects? From short-term episodes of coal dust blown from passing trains to long-term global dispersion and extreme climate change. Soon after the flooding, my oldest eastern Kentucky friend sent me a *New York Times* article partly about this history of environmental disaster. It begins by describing the impact of mining: "Treeless land that is left behind, if not carefully restored, can increase the speed and volume of rain runoff, worsening floods in the mountains."[1] The article goes on to talk about a region that has been a store of commodities and wealth for others. The same can't be said for the people who live here. Betsy Whaley, in an August 2022 report on NPR's *All Things Considered*, says that the decline of coal mining has led to mass layoffs in the mountains, and that many have pulled up stakes. She worries that climate change, which makes inland flooding like that of July 2022 even worse, is creating yet another challenge for the region. She fears that such disasters will mean people abandoning their home places altogether. As Perry County school superintendent Jonathan Jett says, also on *All Things Considered*, "The unfortunate part is some of the communities hit by the flooding were some of the most impoverished." He worries that this disaster could be the final straw for many who have lived here for generations. "I think people if they leave here, they're never coming back."'

* * *

One of my early memories is a long ride from Kentucky to South Bend, Indiana. The year before, Granny and Pa, my mother's parents, had followed my aunt Ruth and her husband, Dave, along with my uncle Roy and his then wife, Betty, in their move to Indiana to work factory jobs. I remember only a little about that trip to Indiana. My father and mother were quarreling again, this time because my father wanted to head to Florida on a deep-sea fishing expedition with his buddy Chappy. My mother couldn't imagine days alone at some motel, so he left us at my grandparents' trailer in the park on the outskirts of South Bend. I remember a patio, the sound of my patent leather shoes scuffing on the concrete, as I stood with my face against my granny's soft, round belly while my parents said goodbye. "I can't believe you're leaving us like this," my mother said. The truth was, she was happiest, and they were happiest with each other, when she was at home with her family, whether back in eastern Kentucky or here in Indiana. For my parents, it had always been that way, as if marriage was a scenario in which my father borrowed my mother for a time, then brought her back to her family of origin.

So my grandfather and my uncles came to Indiana for work. I remember words. *Black lung. Benefits.* Back in Kentucky, I'd seen my grandfather's broken false teeth in a glass in the kitchen, and I'd heard talk about where he'd get them fixed and how much that would cost. I remember my aunt Ruth's nonstop menstruation after the birth of my cousin, Greg. I remember ailing backs and fewer jobs for my uncle, who built houses. And South Bend must have had its attractions. For me, it was root beer floats and chili dogs at the Dog and Suds down the road from the trailer park. It was spending two weeks with my granny and pa, watching cartoons on the rabbit-eared television in the living room. The allure for the men was better jobs, union pay. South Bend was one of the leading industrial manufacturers in the Midwest. It meant woolen mills. It meant plants that made braking and starter systems. There was even a Studebaker plant.

Afternoons, while the men were working and my granny was fixing supper, the aunts lit Winstons and talked. It's easy, from my vantage point now, to fill their mouths with dreams. Dreams of more, of moving closer to South Bend or maybe Mishawaka. A little house with a yard big enough for a garden, but not too big. Friday nights and a drive-in movie, and a beauty parlor, and what was that department store, Robertson's? The aunts said there was a discount rack all the time, upstairs. The dreams were moony-eyed. They were full of rolled-up pants and bobby socks and an Elvis song. The dreams were whispers. They were stories about my aunt Ruth's heavy periods, about being pregnant and miscarrying and trying again. The dreams were men's hands, their own hands, too. "I'm going to learn to drive," Aunt Betty said, tapping a cigarette against the pack. Five years later, she was gone for good up north, a dancer in some bar, but that day, I remember what she said: "I'm going to learn to drive, and then we'll see what's what."

* * *

Used to be, I'd drive home through southwestern Virginia and on into eastern Kentucky on Highways 23 and 119. I'd pass the little town my granny lived in when she was a kid. *Jenkins.* Jenkins was a coal camp when her daddy, Willie May, worked the mines. I'd drive north past Virgie and on to Pikeville, passing other holes in the road that used to be coal camps, and I'd always remember the people I grew up with, many of them miners. Grandfather, uncles, cousins, neighbors. *Leroy, Roy, Dave, Greg, Clifford.* Theirs was the language of coal miners. *Deep. Black damp. Cage. Eye.* And I grew up knowing the words for what mining did to the body. Pa, my mother's father, suffered from black lung. My uncle Roy, when asked about mining, had little to say except that he'd learned that his legs wouldn't let him crawl. Clifford, a neighbor, was down because of his back for good and living on disability. The same *New York Times* article describes a workforce that has been dependent on mining for jobs: "Fewer than half of the adults in Letcher County are in the labor force, and more than a quarter of people under 65 report having a disability. The median household income is about half of the national. The median home value is just $54,700."

Jenkins, Blackey, Virgie. All those former coal camps I'd drive through to get home to Floyd County seemed like ghost towns—a windy two-lane, shut-down storefronts, nothing much there, a fact. Once the coal companies left, such towns made up a population of small communities throughout the mountains. Again, as that *New York Times* piece describes, "the landscape that was built to serve this work was fragile, leaving the people here extraordinarily vulnerable, especially after the coal industry shuttered so many of the mines and moved on. What remained were modest, unprotected homes and decaying infrastructure, and a land that, in many places, had been shorn of its natural defenses."

I was miles away. I was safe. I didn't drive those roads after the recent catastrophic floods that Kentucky's governor Andy Beshear described as the deadliest of a generation. What I've seen are photographs. It's been called a thousand-year flood: a flood with a one in one thousand chance of occurring in any given year. I've seen photographs of brown water rising to rooftops. Water covering gravel access roads up hollows. Miles of debris and the remains of livelihoods. People in deep water, clinging to fallen trees. Rowboats crowded with families. Faces of terrified children. Forty-four lives lost, hundreds missing, thousands of homes destroyed, businesses and jobs lost. A catastrophe, as my grandparents would have said, of Biblical proportions.

As one Letcher Country flood survivor described for the *New York Times* as he looked at the remains of homes, crushed cars, and endless debris, he thought about the effects of such catastrophic loss. "We're gradually losing it—that bond we had. It's slipping away. People are getting out of here, trying to get better jobs and live better lives. I'm leaning in that direction myself."

* * *

Leaving is metaphorical, spiritual. It's hard truth, and its often an insurmountable desire. My cousin Greg once tried to rob a train he hopped on its way to West Virginia, a bandanna over his face and a water pistol he pretended was a gun in his pocket. My cousin Jennie answered a personal ad and moved away to be part of a dominance-and-submission family in Cincinnati. And there were other kinds of leaving. My mother kept a Kentucky driver's manual on the coffee table for twenty years, always claiming she'd learn to drive and go who knew where, though she never did. My aunt Ruby used to walk miles up the highway through Prestonsburg, stopping for coffee at Jerry's Restaurant, and then walking the miles back to the group home where she spent her last years. Greg shot himself in the back room at his mother's trailer. Jennie's daughter took bottles of pills and never made it out of rehab.

I'm the first in my family to pull up roots. I left home at fifteen, pregnant and then raw-edged and angry when I surrendered my son. By nineteen, I'd left a marriage, a trailer, and two apartments. I'd left jobs as a convenience store clerk, a fast-food worker, a maid, a secretary. I moved west, east, south, north. I left houses, towns, cities. Studied, learned, became a whole other person. I left lovers and dogs and cats behind. I hiked canyons and rode Greyhounds. Hitchhiked and slept on borrowed sofas. I left the country, this country, that country. I was a traveler, a wandering spirit, a lost soul.

When I made my way back home again, my grandfather, Pa, wondered when all that education would start working on me. My uncle Dave wondered if I thought I was better than him, and this cut deep. I had no idea what *better than* really meant, and I felt *less than* more often than not. I'd left a trail of destruction in my own wake. I held the syllables of my own name in my mouth, turning them over and over like they could take me somewhere I'd better know who I was and why.

* * *

The word *diaspora* comes from the Greek word διασπορά, meaning "dispersion." Diaspora is forced movement. A scattering, like
seeds cast into the wind. I think of diaspora when I see the haunted
Depression-era photographs of Dorothea Lange, documenting the
1930s migration of families west to California, seeking farmwork
along the way to new lives. I think of diaspora when I see the 1930s
photographs taken by Doris Ulmann when she accompanied John
Jacob Niles as they documented people from the Appalachians.
The photos are about the work of their hands, the work of voices
and songs. They are about home and an undefined elsewhere that
seems to haunt the photographed faces. I think of diaspora when I
remember my own grandmother's face as she stood at the kitchen
window in that Indiana trailer. I imagine she was dreaming of what
Indiana might make of the lives of her children. I imagine she was also
dreaming of Dwale and the garden she'd once had, the tomatoes and
potatoes, the hot sun as she bent, hoed, worked the land she loved.

For my grandmother, home meant the five-room house she lived
in after she married. Home was the place my mother was raised.
It was a garden she didn't especially love, a well with sulfur water
that made her hair coarse. My father took her off to Kansas to be an
air force wife, a life that left her mourning home. Dwale is the land
of my ancestors. Dwale is the memory of my grandmother's hands
as she broke up beans, as she combed my hair, as she watched me
sit on the rocking chairs on the front porch and dream of all the
highways I'd someday take, my personal diaspora away from the
homeplace of generations.

* * *

When I think of my grandmother as she looked out the window of
the trailer in South Bend, Indiana, and dreamed of home, when I

think of the faces of migrants heading west in Dorothea Lange's photographs, or when I think of the faces of Doris Ulmann's mountain people, I think the definitions of diaspora are perhaps inadequate. The Greek word διασπορά means "scattering" or "dispersion." It means me, young and sleeping on a white sand beach on the Greek island of Santorini while furious windstorms called the meltemi swept in from across the Aegean.

Paul and I spent those wind-ridden nights huddled together in a tent set up under a tamarind tree. The winds were sharp-tongued, full of grit and sand, but they would be, Paul said, a chance to see the sand wiped clean. I liked the notion of everything being wiped clean, especially the country-by-country disintegration of our relationship. But the beach was not swept clean. It was strewn with debris. Branches and shells and stones and debris from tourists were here, there, everywhere. *Pamphlets. One sandal. A Styrofoam cup. Half a map.*

One morning while Paul was still sleeping, I made my way down to the water and stripped off my clothes. Just before I waded into the warm blue sea, I touched my hair and ears. I felt the absence of one earring. The earrings were nothing special, just cheap metal and blue glass from a Kentucky thrift store, but I'd worn them for months. The missing thing made my heart race. I checked the water's edge, retraced the steps I'd taken from the tent. I paced the sand where we'd sat the night before as the winds of the meltemi rose. I made bigger and bigger circles, kicking the sand back, picking up handfuls of it and checking, rechecking in my growing panic. Paul was awake by then, and he trailed after me, helped me search, then picked up his own handful of sand, tossed it at me playfully. "You and your silly earring," he said after a bit. Then he waded into the sea and was soon nothing but a blip in the water as the sun rose.

This story is about sleeping on a beach in a windstorm. It's about two years of trekking, thumbing rides, working grape harvests, and climbing mountain peaks. All those things haunt my dreams these years later and make lovely photographs I can take out and hold up to the window as I wish for that kind of distance, escape from my present life. But the real story of that missing earring is a word. *Diaspora. Διασπορά.* I hear the word hiss between my teeth like wind and sand. I say it and think about lost generations. Lost countries. Lost cities, towns, patches of earth this people or that people once worked and lost, lost and couldn't get back. *Scattered. Set wandering.* I see myself digging through the sand on a stretch of Santorini beach, searching for the piece of home those earrings meant. Me, digging a hole to a home on the other side of the world.

* * *

In photos of the July 2022 eastern Kentucky floods, there are eaves of roofs just visible above the risen waters. Photos of four lost children, swept away from the branches of a tree where the family climbed to escape the torrents. Photo of a girl on a rooftop, holding a basin with her little dog inside, both of them hoping for rescue. Lost businesses, lost houses, ravaged land. I felt so much grief as I looked at those photos, I hardly knew who I was anymore. Ten hours away from the place that made me, far from the people who made me, most of them now passed on. *Aunts, uncles, mother, father, cousins.* Haints, all of them. Will-o'-the-wisps I glimpse at night in my dreams of other times, now-gone places. The flood swept away a world already swept away, but I looked at the faces of strangers, and their grief lodges in my heart.

Is there a way back home for those who have lost everything? That *New York Times* article describes sixty-four-year-old Bill Rose as he shoveled his way out of the mounds of mud outside his mechanic shop in Fleming-Neon, Kentucky. It's a shop where he and his brother have long worked on old cars. He and the brother, he says, are committed to staying in the place that raised them. People, he says, have resilience. "You build back," he said. The photo of him in front of his destroyed shop showed him in his waders, mired in mud hip-deep. It showed him with his sleeves rolled up, a tire iron in his filthy hands. "Come hell or high water," he likely said. I think of the far distance of the photograph and some pile of things he'd gathered—hub caps, tools, tires—things found and harbored, a stay against all that had been and still might be. There are words like resilience, perseverance, and I want to give them to Bill Rose and to all the others like him who are still trying to rebuild their lives. I'm not sure such words are or ever can be enough, but I say them again and again, an insufficient offering. "You build back," Bill Rose said.

* * *

In a book called *The Sacred and the Profane*, philosopher and theologian Mircea Eliade describes *axis mundi* as any sacred place that connects heaven to earth, gods to humans. It is a sacred, spiritual, or holy center on earth. I tell myself I've seen such places. In a stream behind the Taj Mahal, where I saw a dead man floating past. In the tree houses of a Thai rainforest, those small, raised temples where monks meditate. Or in the photographs of women, their faces stunned as they sift through an eastern Kentucky flood's aftermath, trying to catch hold of all that's left. *Axis mundi.* A center to catch hold of in times of flux, the chaos of everything.

Maybe it's the only question to ask when seeing a mudflat stretching miles, when wondering what is left. I think of being on a stretch of beach, looking for a lost treasure from home, dreaming of worlds I'd traveled and worlds I'd left behind. I think of Nethaladia at twilight, standing by a hillside, thinking of the fetch and carry, the haul and make-do of her life, right before boulders tumbled down. I think of my grandmother, standing beside a concrete patio in Fort Wayne, Indiana, wanting so badly to bend down, grab a fistful of Kentucky earth. Family after family watched the world sweep past in the waters of a monumental Kentucky flood, wanting nothing so much as to reach out, take hold again. What's left when everything has been lost? When worlds are scattered? I've heard the prayers. *Tell us we can rebuild. Tell us we can have home back again.* They're so little, and so much, but I think of them all the time. Words, mere words, sacred words. I have to believe they matter.

NOTE

1. Rick Rojas, Christopher Flavelle, and Campbell Robertson, "How Coal Mining and Years of Neglect Left Kentucky Towns at the Mercy of Flooding," *New York Times*, August 4, 2022.

SPIRIT HOUSE

RIVER

I saw my first spirit houses with Paul as we rode in a boat along the Chao Phraya River in Bangkok. We floated past temples and markets, past docks and hawkers' stalls, past high-rise malls and the keen notes of Thai pop music. The boat slowed, and we sat in the harsh sun, looking at the iron gates surrounding a huge terraced garden. Inside was a many-storied, many-windowed dwelling and on each side of it, mounted on tall pillars, were two miniature houses. "Guardians," our guide said, his hands raised, palm to palm. "They watch over the spirits of the living." Paul's camera clicked for the house that guarded wealth, again for the house that blessed ancestors. Inset with red, blue, yellow, and silver glass, the spirit dwellings sparkled in the harsh light burning its way through the smog of Bangkok.

GET YOU ONE

I used to have a small blue spirit house that I bought at a roadside sale in eastern Kentucky. The sale included clothes and tools, baked goods, and record albums. The table I stopped at was laden with little handmade houses—bright colors, some covered in moons and stars. As I walked the length of the table, I thought they were birdhouses. A man selling them had one eye and a voice that held a laugh as he picked up a red-and-yellow house and held it out to me. "You can hold them houses up to the wind and about hear your people pray," he said.

SPIRIT INSIDE

After Linda died in the early months of the pandemic, I helped with clearing out her room. I had met Linda a couple of years back while walking my dog, and we developed a friendship over coffee and conversations about Mark, her boyfriend of some twenty years. Mark didn't care that Linda had no resources of her own. Mark didn't care that Linda couldn't work, and he failed to grasp what a stroke meant. Partial paralysis on her left side. Fear of being alone in the dark. The room Linda rented after Mark kicked her out when he met someone new was ten by nine, with just a bed. On the free space on the floor, we found plates with half-eaten sandwiches, unopened Hostess pies. A closet was packed with everything, including a spirit house. It was a sculpture made of barnwood I remembered seeing in Linda's former flower garden. I took it home with me for my own garden. I still think about how it captured her spirit during those pandemic days. Linda, huddled up in the bed with her laptop, streaming soap operas, story after story where everything works out in the end.

PHUKET

By the time we reached southern Thailand, Paul and I had been traveling for almost a year—France, Greece, Australia, India—travels with no more purpose than the next town, the next country. We'd walked the humid districts of Bangkok, bought discount CD players and headphones to resell when we reached India. We'd quarreled about the best money-changing rate as we slept in cheap and good guesthouses. We took a bus north to Chiang Mai, found a hostel that looked across the river to Myanmar. There, we ate blood-streaked eggs from the mangy hens that ran in a yard. We lay beneath the mosquito netting over our separate beds as our quarrels grew and grew alongside our plans.

In southern Thailand, in Phuket, we rented a grass hut by the sea. I walked miles. I swam out to the tall rock formations rising from the ocean, my fingers lingering on sea algae and the mouths of anemones. I hiked into the rainforest, past a tree house where a monk had left his orange robe. In a Buddhist temple, I asked questions of the monks, and I prayed to no one particular god. I knelt before burning incense and photographs of surgeries—bodies cut open at chest or abdomen, missing eyes or limbs. Nuns knelt in prayer as if the photos were offerings to the divine. Come dusk, I made my way back to the grass hut, where we ate bowls of salty dumplings. At night, with the hut's windows propped open to the stifling air, we touched as little as possible.

I recalled what I had asked in the temple. "How do I find the middle of myself?" I asked a monk with a bowl into which I laid two bahts. "There is nothing I can tell you," he said, "that you cannot find inside your own breath." I slept, letting my breath travel in ways I had not. It traveled along a path near the sea, next to smooth boulders and whorl-leaved she-oaks. My breath reached a garden fragrant with jasmine, traveled until it stopped beside a house no bigger than a spread-wide palm. My breath entered the windows of that small spirit house, swept the tiny floors clean. My breath laid its hands against the small bare walls. Like that, I dreamed I traveled west. I crossed continents and oceans. My breath was not as afraid as I myself was of finding a place called home.

NAMES OF SPIRIT HOUSES

Smokehouse. Canning house. Chicken coop. Warm house. Long-house. Hogpen. Coal shed. House at Lynch. House at Lancer. House in Allen. House in Dwale. House in Hagerhill. House in Mining Hollow. House in Prestonsburg. House in Paintsville. Brown house. White house. Green-and-white trailer house. House with a fireplace where the coal ghosts travel up in smoke. House with a trunk found behind a wall. House with glass-eyed dolls. House with quilts. House of the Holy Spirit. House of the Resurrection. House of voices raised in praise. House after the flood. House of bones. House forgotten. House remembered. House that travels through time. Goodbye house. House of my heart. House now that can never be house then.

ABANDONED HOUSE

On the road to Assateague National Park in Virginia, there's a field where I once photographed an abandoned house. Two-storied, used to be white, with broken windows and a door off its hinges, a roof sliding off into the grass. I kicked at tin cans near a rusted barrel full of trash and put an old blue iodine bottle in my pack.

Inside, the house had been visited by William Blake. My phone lit up walls glowing with red and black and yellow shapes. UFOs and aliens and devils. Power fists and words. *Art makes right. Deconstruct this.* Skinny red angels floated down a long hall with a broken window at its end. Through it came the sound of a meadow, bees, and the call of ocean birds. In a bedroom, a rusted bed frame was like one at a grandmother's house when I was little. I remembered jumping on that bed, the giving and creaking of springs. I wondered if spirit ancestors still inhabited this house or if they had long since been called to some other place.

HUNGER

Ghosts residing in Thai spirit houses are hungry, and they are left offerings as appeasement. Coconuts. Bananas. Sticky rice and custard. Once, at the end of a trash-strewn alley in the center of Bangkok, I saw a simple spirit house made of woven straw and tin scraps. On its plywood platform, someone had left rice cakes and brown eggs and syrupy mango slices. Traffic and a tangle of street voices sounded as I knelt. In the midst of the offerings was a burner, an unlit stick of incense, and a small photograph. A girl-child was in the arms of a woman with haunted eyes. At the foot of the photo, an opened can of red Fanta soda. Red soda, I read later, is the equivalent of a blood offering.

WHERE SPIRITS RESIDE

On the top of the shelf in my bedroom is an altar. Objects I love. A piece of jade. Shells from Assateague. Tiny clay cups and a tiny bowl filled with pebbles from Alaska. There are representations of the Holy Mother. Black Madonna from Spain. Hand-carved Mary from Turkey. From Russia, a small icon of Mary and her son. And there are holy photographs. My great-grandmother Beck, sitting in a booth at the Black Cat diner, smoking her pipe. My father, his arm draped across my shoulders, that time I did my first public reading . . . His mother, my mother, her mother, her mother before her.

Below the altar, shelves are crammed with books. Poetry. Volumes on magic and the occult. Meditations. Thomas Merton's *Seven Storey Mountain* is there, as is Rilke's *Book of Hours.* There's *Women of the Golden Dawn. The Tibetan Book of the Dead.* A King James Bible. When I was a child, I wrote the names of those born and of those who'd passed in that Bible. As years turn into decades, I am less sure about what names are left to write down. Mothers and grandmothers, fathers and daughters. And all these shall pass away.

THINGS SPIRITS HAVE BLESSED

Magnifying glass. Kerosene lamp. 78 rpm records. Crochet hooks. Lace doilies. Milking stool. Trip around the World Quilt. Lead crystal perfume bottle. Cast iron kettle. Iodine bottle. Carved wooden saltshakers. *Hagerhill Community Cookbook.* Garnet wedding ring, band worn. Log Cabin Quilt. Straight razor with an ivory handle. Band saw. Deed to forty acres. Candlewick saucers. Small knife, blade thin as paper. Wedding Ring Quilt. Rusty steel cheese grater. Green glass lemon juicer. Embroidered pillowcases. Wooden-handled hammer. Needle, thread, scissors, cloth. A windup mantel clock that no longer works.

SOUP BOWL

I came back to the United States with my backpack stuffed full. Folded inside my T-shirts were stones and bones and feathers from France and Greece. From India there were two papier-mâché boxes from Kashmir, sandstones from Agra, a pair of camel-hair slippers from Rajasthan. From Thailand there was only one gift—a beautiful blue-and-white lidded soup tureen.

These days, I visit my stepmother, who lives alone since my father died, and we watch movies with happy endings. When she goes in to take her evening bath, I look at her curio cabinet, full of her sacred objects. Photos of her grandfather. Stuffed animals. A brush for lathering a face. At the bottom of the curio cabinet is that soup tureen from Thailand, and I take it out, hold it like a talisman. I bought it in a high-rise super mall in Bangkok, found it on a table laden with silk scarves, animal carvings, and miniature paintings of Phuket and Chiang Mai.

I take its gold-edged lid off and peer down into the tureen, thinking about how it's never been used, never held spicy broths and shrimp, glassy noodles and garlic and vegetables. It's a keepsake. I reach inside, feel the cool china sides. The bottom of the tureen seems endless. I reach and reach, and my hand disappears, then my arm, and I let all of me follow. I am a spirit, following a china path back and back. I step into air, into sky. I am standing in my spirit self at the steps leading into a temple with a golden Buddha.

I am holding Paul's hand, and it feels dry and rough, though he, too, will have become nothing but spirit. Spirits, we listen to the chants of monks, the singing bowls that invite us to make ourselves comfortable.

GRAVES

In Prestonsburg, on the way toward Lancer, is a community cemetery. There are gravestones for Leroy and Pearlie Baisden. For Ruby Lafferty. Up Mining Hollow, at a smaller family cemetery, there's Ruth, Dave, and Greg Campbell. Off 23, toward Paintsville, there's another cemetery where my mother, Pearlie Lee Baisden lies. Outside Paintsville, another family cemetery and a proliferation of wild roses. There lie Fanny and Clarence Ida Mae Salyer and John Salyer. Up the holler outside East Point, there are graves I don't even know. Great-grandfather. Great-grandmother. And in the waters of Dewey Lake, at Jenny Wiley, the ashes of my father, Clarence Edsel Salyer. When I visit that lake, I stand outside at night and watch the moonrise. I make myself listen to the barking of dogs. An owl. A whippoorwill. Spirits glad to be spirits.

THE BODY

In the hall, I stand in front of the mirror, studying my naked body. From the walls, photos of my ancestors whisper and laugh. They point out how my body is changing. Breasts descending, stomach a soft pouch, hips rounder. My hands show the years of jobs, of shovel and rake, and I see Willy May, my great-grandfather, in those hands. My face, wrinkles on the forehead, shadows beneath the eyes. That's my mother's. Ghost of her smile in my smile, her laughter rising from my throat. Look at yourself, the spirits say. I fear this aging body, but I look.

Mine is a body gone from the land of its ancestors for more years than it can count. Forty years' journey away from home. Daughter of Pearlie from Dwale and Clarence Edsel from Allen, this body wanted more. Wanted distant countries, towns, cities. Wanted highways and interstates that led away and away. Where the body came from became a dim light on a front porch. Became the memory of a voice in the dark calling me home. This body has forgotten the substance of kith and kin. The open arms to welcome this stranger home have become fewer and fewer. You are becoming, the spirits say, a vessel for what is missing.

Cool air from a vent blows down on my skin. I want to believe that air is palpable, a thing I can grab hold of, release when I want. I want to believe that spirits are not things at all but signs of the lives before us, the lives we have lived and will live, forever and forever, amen. My hands catch air, bring the sweet taste to my mouth. The air is full of spirits, so many I have known and loved, so many I have loved without knowing. Mother, father, uncles, aunts. I take them inside me, one by one by one. I give them the only house I have for now.

ACKNOWLEDGMENTS

Thanks to the editors of the publications where these essays first appeared:

Appalachian Heritage: "Stella, in the Upstairs Room."
Cutleaf: "How Souls Travel."
Fearless: Women's Journeys to Self-Empowerment, Mountain State Press: "Now and Then."
Lit/South Award for Creative Nonfiction: "And Then the Holy River" (previously titled "In Varanasi").
Orison Anthology Award for Creative Nonfiction: "Blue Glass."
Texas Review: "Vertige."

So much gratitude to all those fine folks at and affiliated with the University Press of Kentucky who have helped to foster this work: Ashley Runyon. Abby Freeland. Jackie Wilson. Kousalya Krishnamoorthy.

I am grateful to so many people over time, in no particular order, for their clear-eyed, deeply felt comments on these essays: Annie Woodford, Gordon Johnston, Jason Howard, Prentiss Clark, Carlyle Poteat, Leslie Rindoks, Chris McGinley, Beth Copeland, Cindra Halm, Gwendolyn Turnbull, Ardith Brown, Virginia Craighill, Vicky Hayes.

Thanks for the time spent teaching writing at the University of South Dakota in Vermillion. Those Wednesday evening seminars. Those Friday evenings of music at Cary's. They fed my spirit.

With great appreciation to the University Press of Kentucky and Abby Freeland for believing in this work and listening to its pages.

Many thanks to Marjy Plant, garden master, musician. You've helped me with my garden while I wrote, and the memory of the house concert still inspires me.

So much love to all my friends over these years. You've encouraged me when I've needed it most. You've listened again and again. You've reassured me, drunk wine with me, laughed with me, comforted me. You've welcomed me to your hearths, your tables, and your hearts.

And you, Johnny Johns. No words suffice. Thank you for always being there.

ABOUT THE AUTHOR

John Johns

Karen Salyer McElmurray is the author of *Wanting Radiance: A Novel* and the AWP Creative Nonfiction award-winning memoir and National Book Critics Circle Notable Book *Surrendered Child: A Birth Mother's Journey.* Her essays have won the Annie Dillard Prize, the New Southerner Literary Prize, the *Orison Anthology* Award, the Lit/South Award, and have several times been notable in *Best American Essays.* She has received numerous other awards, including grants from the National Endowment for the Arts, the North Carolina Arts Council, and the Kentucky Foundation for Women and is a visiting writer and lecturer at a variety of programs and reading series.